Propel Your PLC at Work®

Leadership and Coaching Activities for Enriching the Process

ROB J. MEYER

Solution Tree | Press

Copyright © 2025 by Solution Tree Press

All rights reserved, including the right of reproduction of this book in whole or in part in any form.

555 North Morton Street
Bloomington, IN 47404
800.733.6786 (toll free) / 812.336.7700
FAX: 812.336.7790

email: info@SolutionTree.com
SolutionTree.com

Printed in the United States of America

Library of Congress Cataloging-in-Publication Data

Names: Meyer, Rob J., author.
Title: Propel your PLC at Work : leadership and coaching activities for enriching the process / Rob J. Meyer.
Other titles: Propel your professional learning community at work
Description: Bloomington, IN : Solution Tree Press, [2025] | Includes bibliographical references and index.
Identifiers: LCCN 2024041409 (print) | LCCN 2024041410 (ebook) | ISBN 9781962188616 (paperback) | ISBN 9781962188623 (ebook)
Subjects: LCSH: Professional learning communities. | Team learning approach in education. | Teaching teams. | Educational leadership. | School improvement programs. | School management teams.
Classification: LCC LB1731 .M524 2025 (print) | LCC LB1731 (ebook) | DDC 371.1--dc23/eng/20241106
LC record available at https://lccn.loc.gov/2024041409
LC ebook record available at https://lccn.loc.gov/2024041410

Solution Tree
Jeffrey C. Jones, CEO
Edmund M. Ackerman, President

Solution Tree Press
President and Publisher: Douglas M. Rife
Associate Publishers: Todd Brakke and Kendra Slayton
Editorial Director: Laurel Hecker
Art Director: Rian Anderson
Copy Chief: Jessi Finn
Senior Production Editor: Tonya Maddox Cupp
Copy Editor: Charlotte Jones
Text and Cover Designer: Julie Csizmadia
Acquisitions Editors: Carol Collins and Hilary Goff
Content Development Specialist: Amy Rubenstein
Associate Editors: Sarah Ludwig and Elijah Oates
Editorial Assistant: Anne Marie Watkins

Acknowledgments

I feel very honored you are taking time to learn about and use this compilation of learning activities to propel your understanding of the PLC at Work® process. Writing this book has been a journey, and I have many people to thank. First, I want to thank all the architects of the PLC at Work process. This content is not original to me. Rick DuFour, Rebecca DuFour, Bob Eaker, Mike Mattos, Thomas Many, and many others have laid out the blueprint for PLC at Work from which these activities are built.

Second, I want to thank the many mentors from whom I have been fortunate to learn in my professional career. These include principals who have mentored me, leaders who believed in me, superintendents who gave me opportunities to implement the PLC at Work process (thank you, Tonya and Mark!), professional educators who have allowed me to learn alongside them, and my fellow Solution Tree associate friends who have helped develop my knowledge in PLC at Work. I would like to specifically mention Joe Schroeder and Tammy Gibbons from the Association for Wisconsin School Administrators for providing learning opportunities and inspiration that have been pivotal in my growth.

Last, I must thank my family. They make me better each day and have been supportive of this endeavor. Thank you! A bonus thanks to my little brother, Gregory "Bubba" Meyer, who inspired me to "go for it" and do big things. I hope you are smiling, little brother.

Solution Tree Press would like to thank the following reviewers:

Doug Crowley
Assistant Principal
DeForest Area High School
DeForest, Wisconsin

Janet Gilbert
Principal
Mountain Shadows Elementary School
Glendale, Arizona

Justin Heinold
Principal
New Prairie High School
New Carlisle, Indiana

Teresa Kinley
Humanities Teacher
Calgary, Alberta

Brad Neuendorf
Principal
Lander Valley High School
Lander, Wyoming

Janel Ross
Principal
White River School District
Buckley, Washington

Visit **go.SolutionTree.com/PLCbooks** to download the free reproducibles in this book.

Table of Contents

Reproducible pages are in italics.

About the Author ix

Introduction 1

How to Use This Book 2   Where to Start 3

Chapter One
Foundational PLC at Work Concepts 5

Understanding Foundational PLC
at Work Concepts 5

Activities 10

*Topic Processing: Foundational PLC
at Work Concepts* 13

*Analyzing the Current Reality: Foundational
PLC at Work Concepts* 14

Scenarios: Foundational PLC at Work Concepts ... 15

*Scenarios: Foundational PLC at Work
Concepts Key* 17

Plus/Delta: Example Four Pillars 19

Plus/Delta: Example Four Pillars Key 21

Doing the Work: Practicing the Four Pillars 23

Chapter Two
Teams — 25

Understanding Team Structures in a PLC at Work 25	Scenarios: Teams Key 36
Activities 28	Matching: Responsibilities and Teams 38
Topic Processing: Teams 32	Matching: Responsibilities and Teams Key 39
Analyzing the Current Reality: Teams 33	Doing the Work: Writing Team Roles 40
Scenarios: Teams 34	Doing the Work: Writing Team Roles Key 41

Chapter Three
Collaborative Teams — 43

Understanding the Collaborative Team's Role . 43	Ranking: Effective Teams 56
Activities 46	Ranking: Effective Teams Key 57
Topic Processing: Collaborative Teams 50	Doing the Work: Critical Considerations of a Collaborative Team 58
Analyzing the Current Reality: Collaborative Teams 51	Doing the Work: Critical Considerations of a Collaborative Team Key 59
Scenarios: Collaborative Teams 52	
Scenarios: Collaborative Teams Key 54	

Chapter Four
Critical Question One — 61

Understanding Critical Question One 61	Scenarios: Critical Question One in a PLC at Work 70
Activities 64	Scenarios: Critical Question One in a PLC at Work Key 72
Topic Processing: Critical Question One 68	Hit or Miss: Essential Standards 74
Analyzing the Current Reality: Critical Question One 69	Doing the Work: Critical Question One Example Process 75

Chapter Five
Critical Question Two — 77

Understanding Critical Question Two 77	Scenarios: Critical Question Two in a PLC at Work Key 88
Activities 80	Thumbs-Up or Thumbs-Down: Critical Question Two in a PLC at Work 90
Topic Processing: Critical Question Two 84	Thumbs-Up or Thumbs-Down: Critical Question Two in a PLC at Work Key 91
Analyzing the Current Reality: Critical Question Two 85	Doing the Work: Data Analysis 92
Scenarios: Critical Question Two in a PLC at Work 86	

Chapter Six
Critical Question Three — 95

Understanding Critical Question Three	96
Activities	98
Topic Processing: Critical Question Three	102
Analyzing the Current Reality: Critical Question Three	103
Scenarios: Critical Question Three in a PLC at Work	104
Scenarios: Critical Question Three in a PLC at Work Key	106
Determining Actions: Planning How to Respond	108
Determining Actions: Planning How to Respond Key	109
Doing the Work: A Reteaching Plan	110
Doing the Work: A Reteaching Plan Key	111

Chapter Seven
Critical Question Four — 113

Understanding Critical Question Four	113
Activities	116
Topic Processing: Critical Question Four	119
Analyzing the Current Reality: Critical Question Four	120
Scenarios: Critical Question Four in a PLC at Work	121
Scenarios: Critical Question Four in a PLC at Work Key	123
Categorizing: Strategies to Support Intervention and Extension	125
Categorizing: Strategies to Support Intervention and Extension Key	127
Doing the Work: An Extension Plan	129
Doing the Work: An Extension Plan Key	130

Chapter Eight
Teaching-Assessing-Learning Cycle — 133

Understanding the Teaching-Assessing-Learning Cycle	134
Activities	136
Topic Processing: Teaching-Assessing-Learning Cycle	139
Analyzing the Current Reality: Teaching-Assessing-Learning Cycle	140
Scenarios: Teaching-Assessing-Learning Cycle	142
Scenarios: Teaching-Assessing-Learning Cycle Key	144
Matching: Teaching-Assessing-Learning Cycle Components	146
Matching: Teaching-Assessing-Learning Cycle Components Key	148
Doing the Work: Planning a Teaching-Assessing-Learning Cycle	150
Doing the Work: Planning a Teaching-Assessing-Learning Cycle Key	152

Epilogue — 155

References and Resources — 157

Index — 161

About the Author

Rob J. Meyer, EdD, is an experienced educator currently serving as the director of teaching and learning at Beaver Dam Unified School District in Wisconsin. With more than eighteen years in education, he previously served as a teacher of social studies, an assistant principal at the secondary level, and a principal at the primary level. Rob successfully uses the Professional Learning Community (PLC) at Work® process to improve outcomes for the students he serves. By focusing on a districtwide effort to implement research-based systems of continuous improvement, he helped improve data across sites, which led to a Model PLC at Work school designation in his district.

As someone who believes in the power of collaboration, Rob is a past president of Wisconsin ASCD. Additionally, he has presented at several conferences on educational leadership and mentored instructional leaders.

Rob received a bachelor's degree in broadfield social studies with a minor in history, as well as teacher credentials, from the University of Wisconsin-Stevens Point. He earned a master's degree in educational leadership from Cardinal Stritch University in Milwaukee, Wisconsin. Rob received a superintendent license credential at Edgewood College in Madison, Wisconsin, where he also completed a doctorate in education.

Introduction

> [A professional learning community] is the central organizing principle of successful schools, whatever their demographics.
>
> —DOUGLAS REEVES

If we assume educators have a common desire for the best educational system, we must also assume educators have a common desire to implement what we know works. While research reveals many strategies that positively impact learning, Douglas Reeves (2020) sent a message in *Achieving Equity and Excellence: Immediate Results From the Lessons of High-Poverty, High-Success Schools* by listing schools organizing themselves as a professional learning community (PLC) as the first principle of these high-success schools. It is this process that schools continually implement and refine to reach the highest levels of learning. Some examples of confirmed improved academic and behavioral learning in a school functioning as a PLC follow (DuFour, DuFour, Eaker, Many, Mattos, & Muhammad, 2024, p. 12).

Tanque Verde Unified School District began their journey to implement the PLC at Work process in 2017. In their two elementary schools, the third-grade passing rates on the statewide ELA assessment jumped from 52 to 77 percent and from 60 to 75 percent between 2019 and 2022 (Read On Arizona, 2024).

Fern Creek High School increased its test scores from the bottom 10 percent to the 76th percentile of all Kentucky schools within five years to shed its "persistently low achievement" label (Solution Tree, 2024b, p. 3).

After establishing itself as a PLC, Minnieville Elementary—serving a highly diverse, academically challenging, high English learner population—became the highest-performing Title I school in Prince William County and now boasts a 96 percent passing rate in both ELA and math (Solution Tree, 2024a).

This book, a collection of topics and related activities, is about Professional Learning Communities at Work®. It provides districts, schools, and teams who are orienting themselves to the right work of a PLC at Work with a set of foundational learning activities to propel their understanding, deepening PLC implementation.

While this text can be applied to all educators, again, it is specifically designed to support those who lead or plan professional learning for K–12 districts, schools, or teams. This may be district-level leaders, principals, instructional coaches, or teacher leaders. It provides facilitators with ideas to propel the learning of a PLC at Work for teachers who do the daily work in teams. You should also know that the activities are designed for easy implementation in relatively short time frames. However, you can easily modify activities to embody more interactive, collaborative professional learning strategies.

Because this book is an introductory resource and for professional development, it does not describe every structure a school should implement in depth, nor does it provide detailed descriptions about each action a teacher team should be taking. This text supports the foundational text *Learning by Doing: A Handbook for Professional Learning Communities at Work®*, Fourth Edition (DuFour et al., 2024). While the text you are reading appropriately cites that resource, there are concepts of the PLC at Work process that have become general knowledge and may not be cited as from a specific source. This book organizes some of that information to help readers. Additionally, there are elements of other texts extending this work, such as *Taking Action: A Handbook for RTI at Work,* Second Edition (Mattos, Buffum, Malone, Cruz, Dimich, & Schuhl, 2024) and *Behavior Solutions: Teaching Academic and Social Skills Through RTI at Work* (Hannigan, Hannigan, Mattos, & Buffum, 2021), as these texts provide further understanding and systems for meeting student needs.

How to Use This Book

How you use this text will depend on your role.

- A facilitator, such as a principal, district-level leader, instructional coach, or team leader may use this book to deepen their understanding of a PLC at Work or develop common knowledge.

- New educators or onboarding programs may use this text to become familiar with the PLC process as they immerse themselves in a school or district that is already in the process.

- A whole school may use this text so each staff member can participate in a shared learning experience that helps develop a strong foundational understanding of a PLC at Work. In this instance, it can be used as a participant handbook. In addition, it can be a precursor to other texts that go deeper into particular elements such as assessment, school culture, intervention, or extension.

Each chapter addresses a topic about the PLC at Work concept, deepening the learning. After that, three corresponding activities appear in each chapter. All activities have corresponding participant handouts, and some also have keys for the facilitator only. *This style font indicates what is different on the facilitator key reproducibles.*

- The first activity provides scenarios on the chapter's subject and asks participants to analyze each. They identify what is effective or good practice and what is ineffective or poor practice in each scenario.

- The second activity is specific to the content of the chapter, providing a relevant way to apply learning. These activities also offer readers different professional development ideas over the course of the text that facilitators can adapt and use to support future learning, developing a menu of professional learning activities. While still structured, this activity helps participants reflect on the concept so they may gain a deeper understanding.

- The third activity provides a chance for participants to *do the work* by having them practice skills necessary for the topic. This activity may take longer than the others, and it has fewer scaffolds because it is more open-ended than the other activities. This is intended to segue from learning to replicating the actual site and teamwork.

You will notice repeated instructions if reading this book from cover to cover. This is intentional; it allows users to go directly to chapters or activities without referencing other parts of text.

These activities are not time consuming. Depending on how the facilitator applies them, they can range from five to forty minutes (or so). The ability to customize these activities allows you to use them in collaborative team meetings, staff meetings, induction workshops, and the like. Take each and turn it into the learning that works best for those you support. Each chapter also has "Topic Processing" or "Analyzing the Current Reality" tools.

Where to Start

This text is designed for users to use front to back, to skip around, or to develop a site-level learning development plan. There is certainly versatility. The only wrong way is *not* to use it. The chapter breakdown is as follows: Chapter 1 explains foundational PLC at Work concepts including the three big ideas of a PLC, the four pillars, loose and tight elements, and the four critical questions. Chapter 2 explains the different kinds of teams and what roles they play, and then chapter 3 drills down further into collaborative teams because the collaborative team is the heartbeat of a PLC at Work. Chapters 4 through 7 each study critical questions one through four in turn, and chapter 8 pulls those questions together and places them in the context of the teaching-assessing-learning cycle.

As you read and participate in activities, reflect on two questions.

1. **Are we spending our time on the right work?** Because time is a limited resource, we cannot afford to focus on structures, processes, or strategies that do not yield student growth and achievement. Consider whether or not you, your team, or your school are implementing this process effectively and are ensuring that other principles, which may also be beneficial to student achievement, are built *on* the PLC at Work process rather than in place of it.

2. **What processes and structures are you, your team, or your school already skilled at, and what areas can you identify for growth?** This identification allows you to chart your course. Schools must ensure they perpetuate what is going well while also addressing areas of need. Your course is charted by planning to maintain what is gaining results and addressing what is not. Celebrate the concepts you believe are in place. Celebrating and confirming quality work are important. Then, identify where you can grow and how you will do that. To make this reality, think about who will do what by when. Educational consultant and former principal Kenneth C. Williams (n.d.) often shares that "the answer is in the room". You may need to invest in further professional learning materials, workshops, or consultancy. I share Williams' words, however, to illustrate that your first step can be seeking your colleagues', teams', school leadership's, or mentors' support. Chances are there is someone working alongside you who can help. One day, you will be able to return the favor.

Enjoy the learning!

Chapter One

Foundational PLC at Work Concepts

This chapter explains the foundational elements of a PLC at Work in a broad way. Schools or districts that skip directly to "doing the work" without setting the stage with this knowledge take significantly longer to, or perhaps never, see the results they set out to achieve. This is due to schools skipping crucial steps, such as developing a common mission. It is important to make sure there is a solid understanding of what a PLC is and is not and how to initiate its development.

Understanding Foundational PLC at Work Concepts

A PLC at Work is often misconstrued for a team of teachers who work together in some manner. To be clear, this is not what a PLC is. It is not a meeting, a group of people, or a self-bestowed label. Its designers describe PLC at Work as "an ongoing process in which educators work in recurring cycles of collective inquiry and action research to increase their learning and the learning of the students they serve" (DuFour et al., 2024, p. 2). The key part of this definition is the concept of a *process*. Yes, teachers must work collaboratively. However, they work collaboratively across the system to get better results for students and don't stop.

The idea that a single group of teachers working together could be a PLC misses the bigger picture. Zoom out. Organizing an entire school to focus on the highest levels of learning for all students and constantly pursuing better results using what we know about effective schools through research is much more complicated than a team of teachers working together in some random way. It is the entirety of a system working cohesively toward excellence that makes a PLC.

Do the teacher teams adhere to outlined systems and processes and work toward continuous improvement? If not, they are practicing PLC *lite*, which is indicated by the following five challenges: "(1) a relentless commitment to the status quo, (2) the absence of a guaranteed and viable curriculum, (3) a failure to accurately define success, (4) a focus on 'coblaboration' over collaboration, and (5) a focus on inputs more than outputs" (Reibel, Gobble, Onuscheck, & Twadell, 2024, p. 3).

An entire institution must commit to functioning as an established PLC. A school or district can call itself a PLC if it has committed to and is implementing the research-based structures, processes, and strategies for effective schools (Akiba & Liang, 2016; Anderson & Olivier, 2022; DuFour et al., 2024; Hord, 1997; Reeves, 2020). Some of those structures are the three big ideas of a PLC, the four pillars, loose and tight elements, and the four critical questions.

Three Big Ideas

A PLC is built on three big ideas that focus the work of the entire system. As each idea is discussed, I should remind you that each of these big ideas is based on research into what successful schools have done to continually produce learning at high levels (Reeves, 2020; Hord, 1997, 2015; Simms, 2024, respectively). They are not arbitrary. The three big ideas follow (DuFour et al., 2024).

1. **A focus on learning:** This idea puts forth the concept that everything a school does must be checked against the idea that schools are established to produce high levels of learning for every student. If this is the fundamental purpose, and it is, we must relentlessly pursue it. Consider this when thinking about the first big idea: *Is everything we do oriented to produce learning?*

2. **A collaborative culture and collective responsibility:** This idea is that no one teacher can ensure high levels of learning for every student in the system. Therefore, we must support each other and learn together to improve ourselves and the system for the benefit of the students we serve. Consider this when thinking about the second big idea: *Do we work together to achieve the best outcomes?*

3. **A results orientation:** This idea focuses on monitoring progress. Schools must determine whether what they are doing is leading to the results they wish to achieve or if they need to adjust. Consider this when thinking about the third big idea: *Do we measure our progress in order to learn and adjust?*

All PLC structures relate to putting these three big ideas into action. For example, the collaborative teams at each school site determine clear learning goals (related to big idea one); plan how and when those will be attained (related to big idea two); and then check to make sure that those goals are met while responding to needs through assessments (related to big idea three).

Four Pillars: Mission, Vision, Values, and Goals

Schools in pursuit of the highest levels of learning certainly need to understand the three big ideas. However, these three big ideas need to be digested by and spelled out explicitly for each member of the system. This is where the four pillars come in—an organization's (1) mission, (2) vision, (3) values, and (4) goals (DuFour et al., 2024). The four pillars create the crystal clear picture you need to set off in the right direction. The entire staff collaboratively builds these four pillars to develop clarity and solidarity.

- **Mission:** The mission is a school-level answer to the question, "*Why do we exist?*" (DuFour et al., 2024, p. 47, italics added). Establishing the mission, if we have an understanding of the three big ideas, should declare that we exist to produce high levels of learning for every student.

- **Vision:** The vision answers the question, "*What must our school become to accomplish our purpose?*" (DuFour et al., 2024, p. 47, italics added). In other words, the vision is what we will be down the road when we truly achieve greatness. Establishing the vision collaboratively as a school provides each member of the system the direction they need to relentlessly pursue. Saying where you want to go leads to better outcomes for student growth and achievement through adult practice (Höchli, Brügger, & Messner, 2018). The mission and vision provide this for a school.

- **Values:** Values answer the question, "*How must we behave to achieve our vision?*" (DuFour et al., 2024, p. 47, italics added). Values are the result of collective commitments. While the mission and vision give us purpose and direction, the values provide the behaviors to which everyone commits in order to achieve the mission and vision. These collective commitments for schools are often based on the six tight elements of a PLC. After you determine the mission, vision, and values, you must be able to plan effectively and measure progress. This is where goals come in.

- **Goals:** Goals answer the question, "*How will we mark our progress?*" (DuFour et al., 2024, p. 47, italics added). Schools often have long-term goals they break down into annual goals. Developing goals ensures that everyone is clear about what the current priorities are in the pursuit of the school's vision. In addition to clarity, setting and recording goals increases the chance of succeeding at them (Gardner & Albee, 2015).

Figure 1.1 has an example mission, vision, values, and corresponding goals. Notice that each element is connected. The mission is about coming to work every day to ensure high levels of learning. This mission, pursued, leads to the vision being actualized. In addition, the collective commitments are linked to what is expected in the vision. Last, the goals are representative of the continuous improvement and high expectations presented in the mission, vision, and collective commitments.

Mission: We work relentlessly to ensure that every student achieves at high levels and has a positive experience.

Vision: Our school is focused on improvement to achieve high expectations as we are collaborative, engaged in learning, and have a system that ensures success for all students.

Values (also known as collective commitments): To achieve our mission, vision, and goals, we will:

- Serve on a collaborative team with the united purpose of ensuring high levels of learning for all students
- Develop and continually refine a curriculum that is both meaningful and doable for every course offered to our students
- Use assessments to measure our performance as teachers, developing plans to improve accordingly
- Use assessments to determine the needs of students, providing ongoing extensions and interventions as necessary

Goals:

Goal one: We will ensure every student is prepared for the next grade level in both mathematics and English language arts. We will have an annual SMART goal to track improvement.

Goal two: We will ensure every student feels as though they have a support network within our school. We will have an annual SMART goal to track improvement.

Figure 1.1: Example of mission, vision, values, and goals alignment.

Establishing your mission, vision, values, and goals is the first step in realizing the three big ideas. However, you need structures. Therefore, each member of the PLC must be on a team that has been assembled to achieve the vision. The most common team type in the system is *collaborative teacher teams*, also known as *professional learning teams*. These teams are made up of educators who have a common goal or function. Examples include three teachers who all teach the same course or four teachers who teach *singletons* (courses they are the only ones who teach) yet focus on the same skill goals, such as developing reading, writing, or college and career readiness. You can read more about different team types in chapter 2 (page 25).

Loose and Tight Elements

Schools receive research-based guidance, but individual sites pursue their own journey in the framework. Therefore, some elements are loose, and some are tight. *Loose* elements are those that allow greater flexibility compared to *tight* elements which, in order to ensure success, are musts.

Tight elements are mentioned in relation to values. These elements, which are non-negotiable, follow (DuFour et al., 2024).

- Educators on a collaborative team work in collaborative teams and take collective responsibility, meaning that there is a shared belief in the ability of the adults to work together and meet student needs for student learning.
- They implement a guaranteed and viable curriculum, unit by unit. Such a curriculum *guarantees* that "all teachers who teach the same levels or courses teach the same content. The content students learn does not vary depending on the teachers they are assigned. *Viable* means that the content is teachable in the time available" (Simms, 2024, p. 71).
- They monitor student learning through ongoing, frequent, team-developed formative assessments.
- They use common assessments to do the following.
  ‣ Learn and grow professional practices for every adult
  ‣ Collaborate toward goals and apply learning to future units or learning cycles
  ‣ Decide on and provide student interventions and extensions
- They provide a system of interventions and extensions.

With the tight elements in place, collaborative teams make decisions necessary for student success. The loose elements (DuFour et al., 2024) follow.

- They determine the most important standards and skills that are to be taught.
- They decide on the best order for these standards and skills to be taught as well as the time needed to do so.
- They determine the definition of *proficiency*.
- They develop and plan assessments that will determine student proficiency.
- They decide on norms to help the team function at a high level.
- They develop team goals to focus their work.

Once teams understand the tight and loose elements of a PLC at Work, they are ready to learn about the four critical questions that bring these elements to life by providing more specific team operation guidance.

The Four Critical Questions

These teams, in pursuit of the vision and abiding by the collective commitments, focus their collaborative time on four critical questions, which follow:

1. What knowledge, skills, and dispositions should every student acquire as a result of this unit, this course, or this grade level? [often paraphrased as *What do we want students to know and be able to do?*]
2. How will we know when each student has acquired the essential knowledge and skills? [or, *How will we know if they learned it?*]
3. How will we respond when some students do not learn? [or, *How will we respond if they have not learned it?*]
4. How will we extend the learning for students who are already proficient?

[or, *How will we respond if they already know it?*] (DuFour et al., 2024, p. 44)

Each of these questions can be further broken down into processes. However, at the simplest level, teams must make sure to do the following.

- They must decide what is most important to learn in their units and courses by determining essential standards or learning goals that create a guaranteed and viable curriculum.
- They must understand they will measure that learning by creating common assessments used to determine whether educators are meeting students' needs and who is and is not meeting learning goals.
- They must decide how they will intervene if the desired learning is not achieved and plan to reteach the learning goal in a new way.
- They must determine how they will extend learning when students have achieved the desired learning by pursuing a learning goal at a more complex level.

Organizing the school into collaborative teams that focus on the four critical questions adds a structure to learning by ensuring there are common assessments and monitored results on which teachers act. As you learn more about other teams and structures in a PLC (chapter 2, page 25), you will see how they connect back to the foundational three big ideas.

Other teams also focus on the four critical questions—or, perhaps, a subset of them. For example, the school may have a team that determines the behavioral expectations for students, how the school will monitor behaviors, and how they will intervene when students do not meet those expectations. This is the same process as the collaborative teacher team, but the specifics apply schoolwide.

Discussion Questions and Next Steps Resources

Consider these questions after reading this chapter.

- Before reading, what was your initial impression of a PLC? If you've been working as part of a PLC, what has your impression grown to be?
- If you are new to PLCs, what about your initial impression was confirmed or changed after reading?
- What is either an action step to which you can commit or a question you need to explore based on your understanding of a PLC?

Suggested resources follow that can help you take next steps (if your existing PLC has not yet addressed those elements). These are in addition to the foundational texts mentioned in the introduction.

- Kim Bailey and Chris Jakicic's (2019) *Make It Happen: Coaching With the Four Critical Questions of PLCs at Work*
- Anne E. Conzemius and Jan O'Neill's (2014) *The Handbook for SMART School Teams: Revitalizing Best Practices for Collaboration*, Second Edition
- Richard DuFour, Rebecca DuFour, Robert Eaker, Mike Mattos, and Anthony Muhammad's (2021) *Revisiting PLCs at Work: Proven Insights for Sustained, Substantive School Improvement*, Second Edition
- Mike Mattos, Rebecca DuFour, Richard DuFour, Robert Eaker, and Thomas W. Many's (2016) *Concise Answers to Frequently Asked Questions About Professional Learning Communities at Work*
- Anthony R. Reibel, Troy Gobble, Mark Onuscheck, and Eric Twadell's (2024) *Beyond PLC Lite: Evidence-Based Teaching and Learning in a Professional Learning Community at Work*
- Bob Sonju, Maren Powers, and Sheline Miller's (2023) *Simplifying the Journey: Six Steps to Schoolwide Collaboration, Consistency, and Clarity in a PLC at Work*

Activities

Before moving on to the activities, ask participants to complete the reproducible "Topic Processing: Foundational PLC at Work Concepts" (page 13) to ensure they have a foundational understanding that allows them to apply their learning. Then have participants complete the reproducible "Analyzing the Current Reality: Foundational PLC at Work Concepts" (page 14). It will help you understand the team's implementation and determine what may come next for them. To complete this tool, you may need to ask questions of your team and school leadership.

As the facilitator, you may choose to use one, some, or all of these learning opportunities based on need. In addition, you can modify any activity to meet adult learners' needs and facilitate engaged learning.

- **Scenarios: Foundational PLC at Work Concepts** is intended to help participants think about what it really takes to be a PLC. Everyone reads a scenario and determines what about each is representative of a true PLC and what is *not* representative of, or contradictory to, a PLC by completing a graphic organizer. Each scenario is written so both concepts are evident, allowing participants to reasonably complete the entire graphic organizer. You can modify this activity into a gallery walk or jigsaw; you can also modify the scenarios to fit the audience.

- **Plus/Delta: Example Four Pillars** is intended to help people think about what a mission, vision, set of collective commitments, and set of goals created for a school should or should not include. In this activity, participants evaluate examples of the four pillars. A graphic organizer is provided for participants to record what is positive about the sample (+) and what they would change about the sample (Δ). The facilitator can easily modify the samples to be more representative of their setting or to include local examples. No matter how the samples are presented or modified, the important part is to have a rich discussion in order to develop a deeper understanding.

- **Doing the Work: Practicing the Four Pillars** is intended to deepen the understanding of the four pillars by having people independently draft their own mission, vision, collective commitments, and corresponding goals. In reality, this work is done collaboratively. However, participants practice by recording their own drafts of the four pillars and their rationale for each. You can easily modify this activity, pending audience size, to be completed in collaborative groups which may be more representative of how a school would actually conduct the process.

Facilitating Professional Learning

Make the goal of a professional learning session known.

Don't leave the intended outcomes for participants a mystery. This does not mean you must lead with a learning target or objective, as you may lead with some type of hook to create interest in the learning. What this does mean is that both the facilitator and participants should know the intended outcome. That understanding provides focus and clarity. If the facilitator and audience are both clear about what they are trying to do differently, they are more likely to maintain focus on that goal and achieve it.

Scenarios: Concepts in a PLC at Work

In this activity, participants review scenarios, discuss them, and identify what parts of the scenarios properly represent a PLC at Work and what parts do not. While some of the scenarios may seem obvious, it is the discussion of *why* that makes this learning activity meaningful. If, in these scenarios, participants correctly identify what represents a PLC at Work and what does not, they signify an understanding of the process and have a greater chance for effective implementation.

Follow these steps.

1. Before beginning, ensure some type of professional learning was shared to support the participants' understanding. This may be reading and debriefing this chapter's text.

2. Provide each participant with a copy of "Scenarios: Foundational PLC at Work Concept" (page 15) or display it for all to read. Keep a copy of "Scenarios: Foundational PLC at Work Concepts Key" (page 17) for yourself to support later in the steps.

3. Ensure that each participant has a partner or group to engage with. Cap groups at four people to allow for effective discussion.

4. One round at a time, have participants read a scenario. Participants then, in the What Is Representative of a PLC and What Is *Not* Representative of a PLC columns, record details from the scenarios accordingly. Ask participants to refrain from moving on to the next round when they are done.

5. After each participant has read the scenario and recorded their rationale, they discuss with their partner or group. This can include the facilitator checking for consensus on the rationale and engaging in conversation where there may be disagreement. For example, you may ask for participants to share their answer, the rationale for their answer, and doubts about their answer.

6. If there is more than one group of participants, facilitate a whole-group conversation to see if there is consensus or dissonance on the rationale.

7. Provide the group with the suggested answers from "Scenarios: Foundational PLC at Work Concepts Key" to spur further conversation.

8. Pending the group's answers, further discussion may be needed to provide a deeper understanding of the suggested answers and evidence. For example, if there are significant disagreements or misunderstandings, the facilitator may need to refer to resources on the concept to provide participants additional opportunities to learn.

9. Proceed to the second and subsequent rounds, repeating the process.

Plus/Delta: Example Four Pillars

In this activity, participants will review sample school missions, visions, collective commitments, and goals. For each sample, participants will evaluate the sample and record what is positive or good about it (+) and what they would change to strengthen it (Δ). As with most sample activities, it is the discussion of *why* that makes this learning activity meaningful. The discussion of why, rather than a standard identification, demonstrates thought and learning and requires metacognition.

Follow these steps.

1. Before beginning, ensure some type of professional learning was shared to support the participants' understanding. This may be reading and debriefing this chapter's text.

2. Provide each participant with a copy of "Plus/Delta: Example Four Pillars" (page 19) or display it for all to read. Keep a copy of "Plus/Delta: Example Four Pillars Key" (page 21) for yourself to support discussion.

3. Ensure each participant has a partner or group to engage with. Cap groups at four people to allow for effective discussion.

4. One round at a time, have participants read an example. Participants then, in the What Is Positive About This Example (+) and What You Would Change About This Example (Δ), write correspondingly about

the example. Ask participants to refrain from moving on to the next round when they are done.

5. After each participant has read the example and recorded their responses, they discuss with a partner or group. This can include checking for consensus on their rationale and discussing disagreements.

6. If there is more than one group of participants, facilitate a whole-group conversation to see if there is consensus or dissonance.

7. Provide the group with the suggested answers from "Plus/Delta: Example Four Pillars Key" to spur further conversation.

8. Pending the group's answers, further discussion may be needed to provide a deeper understanding of the suggested answers and evidence. For example, if there are significant disagreements or misunderstandings, the facilitator may need to refer to resources on the concept to provide participants additional opportunities to learn.

9. Proceed to the following rounds, repeating the process.

Doing the Work: Practicing the Four Pillars

In this activity, participants practice writing four pillars of a PLC. While they would do this collaboratively for their school or district to align with PLC processes, and a school is likely to have multiple collective commitments and multiple goals, this activity provides an opportunity to process what these foundations may look like and the chance to reflect on what the school's ideal response might be.

Follow these steps.

1. Before beginning, ensure some type of professional learning was shared to support the participants' understanding. This may be reading and debriefing this chapter's text.

2. Provide each participant with a copy of "Doing the Work: Practicing the Four Pillars" (page 23) or display for all to read.

3. Ensure each participant has a partner or group to engage with. Cap groups at four people to allow for effective discussion.

4. Participants should complete their drafts in the My Draft column based on what they know about the four pillars and on their own beliefs. Then, in the Why I Wrote My Draft This Way column, respond accordingly.

5. After each participant has recorded their responses, they discuss with a partner or group. This can include providing each other affirmations and constructive criticism. To add, you can ask partners and groups to redraft representing the thinking of their group. This could prepare them to start a whole school process of creating the four pillars.

6. If there is more than one group, facilitate a whole-group conversation so that participants can collectively reflect on their experience.

Topic Processing: Foundational PLC at Work Concepts

Is this a success area or a growth area for me, my team, or my school and why?	What are my next steps to grow in my understanding?	Where can I get support to grow?

Propel Your PLC at Work © 2025 Solution Tree Press • SolutionTree.com
Visit **go.SolutionTree.com/PLCbooks** to download this free reproducible.

Analyzing the Current Reality: Foundational PLC at Work Concepts

To complete this tool, you may need to ask questions of your team and school leadership. Doing so will assist your understanding and help you learn what may come next for your team. The evidence column allows you to provide specific evidence of the current reality.

Concept	Current Reality	Evidence
My colleagues know the three big ideas of a PLC.	☐ Not at all true. ☐ Somewhat true. ☐ Mostly true. ☐ Always true.	
My site has established a vision, mission, collective commitments, and goals.	☐ Not at all true. ☐ Somewhat true. ☐ Mostly true. ☐ Always true.	
My site has a process for establishing and pursuing annual goals for bettering student outcomes.	☐ Not at all true. ☐ Somewhat true. ☐ Mostly true. ☐ Always true.	
My team can identify the four critical questions of a PLC.	☐ Not at all true. ☐ Somewhat true. ☐ Mostly true. ☐ Always true.	
My team uses the four critical questions of a PLC as a foundation for collaborative team time.	☐ Not at all true. ☐ Somewhat true. ☐ Mostly true. ☐ Always true.	

Propel Your PLC at Work © 2025 Solution Tree Press • SolutionTree.com
Visit **go.SolutionTree.com/PLCbooks** to download this free reproducible.

Scenarios: Foundational PLC at Work Concepts

Scenario	What Is Representative of a PLC	What Is Not Representative of a PLC
Round one The principal of a school ensures each staff meeting starts with a reading of the school's mission and vision. In addition, progress toward school goals is provided using metrics. School staff have an opportunity to discuss with their peers the successes and next steps they can take to continue pursuing goals.		
Round two The principal of a school decides adult actions in the building need to change in order to improve student outcomes. Therefore, he writes a list of ten actions to which the staff must commit. The principal shares these actions with staff in an in-service meeting. Staff are required to sign off that they commit to these behaviors. Actions include the use of common assessments, committing to using high-leverage practices, and setting professional goals with action plans.		
Round three A middle school decides to focus on improvement in literacy scores. Therefore, the English language arts teachers are provided time to collaborate weekly by grade level. An administrator attends each meeting to ensure these teams of educators use the same unit assessments, analyze the data together, and make plans for improvement based on the assessment results.		

Round four An elementary school establishes a time for teams of teachers to meet. These are set up to meet weekly and usually do. The teams are made up of teachers who teach at the same grade level. The agendas of these teams are usually focused on sharing activities and materials related to the content of the unit of study. Generally, staff find the sharing of activities beneficial.		
Round five A school's leadership team (with representation from across staff) leads the "welcome back" in-service at the beginning of the school year. They review with staff the importance of collaborative teams, team goal setting, prioritizing learning goals, using common assessments, using assessment data to support student needs, and reflecting on adult practices to improve student learning.		

Scenarios: Foundational PLC at Work Concepts Key

Scenario	What Is Representative of a PLC	What Is Not Representative of a PLC
Round one The principal of a school ensures each staff meeting starts with a reading of the school's mission and vision. In addition, progress toward school goals is provided using metrics. School staff have an opportunity to discuss with their peers the successes and next steps they can take to continue pursuing goals.	The mission, vision, goals, and data are a priority. School staff have the opportunity to engage in discussion and plan.	A PLC must be a part of how the school operates and not just what a leader communicates. It appears, to some degree, the principal of the site may be leading the work independently rather than sharing the responsibility with staff.
Round two The principal of a school decides that adult actions in the building need to change to improve student outcomes. Therefore, he writes a list of ten actions to which the staff must commit. The principal shares these actions with staff in an in-service meeting. Staff are required to sign off that they commit to these behaviors. Actions include the use of common assessments, committing to using high-leverage practices, and setting professional goals with action plans.	The principal seems to be in tune with the needs of the school and understands commitments must be made to see improvements. In addition, the actions are aligned to the work of collaborative teams in the PLC process.	The principal does not appear to understand the collaborative nature of the PLC process and has, therefore, operated in a silo and delivered commands to staff without sharing the why or providing support.
Round three A middle school decides to focus on improvement in literacy scores. Therefore, the English language arts teachers are provided time to collaborate weekly by grade level. An administrator attends each meeting to ensure these teams of educators use the same unit assessments, analyze the data together, and make plans for improvement based on the assessment results.	There appears to be evidence of focus, analysis of data, and collaboration. In addition, the collaboration is focused on key actions of collaborative teams.	A PLC is an entire organization. While this scenario has appropriate elements of a PLC, it is limited to one department and is not representative across the school.

Round four	There is evidence teams	A PLC is focused on
An elementary school establishes a time for teams of teachers to meet. These are set up to meet weekly and usually do. The teams are made up of teachers who teach at the same grade level. The agendas of these teams are usually focused on sharing activities and materials related to the content of the unit of study. Generally, staff find the sharing of activities beneficial.	are established and meet regularly with agendas.	learning, collaboration, and results. The work of teams in this scenario is focused on sharing a workload rather than on student learning, teacher collaboration, and student outcomes.
Round five	There is evidence of shared leadership as multiple staff members are leading the in-service. In addition, there is learning among adults focused on key PLC concepts.	A PLC is more than a one-time learning session. While this scenario looks great overall, it is important that there are regular opportunities to engage in adult learning.
A school's leadership team (with representation from across staff) leads the "welcome back" in-service at the beginning of the school year. They review with staff the importance of collaborative teams, team goal setting, prioritizing learning goals, using common assessments, using assessment data to support student needs, and reflecting on adult practices to improve student learning.		

Plus/Delta: Example Four Pillars

Participants should be prepared to explain both why they find their listed positives positive, and why they would change something about the example.

Example	What Is Positive About This Example (+) and Why	What You Would You Change About This Example (Δ) and Why
Round one Mission—Our school mission is to support students so they can learn to the best of their ability.		
Round two Mission—Our school mission is to ensure every student learns at high levels and that we do what it takes to make that happen.		
Round three Vision—Our school vision is to be a place where students want to learn and achieve their goals.		
Round four Vision—Our school vision is to be a collaborative learning community that meets the needs of every student, resulting in high levels of learning.		

Propel Your PLC at Work © 2025 Solution Tree Press • SolutionTree.com
Visit **go.SolutionTree.com/PLCbooks** to download this free reproducible.

Round five Collective commitment—We will work together to achieve school goals.		
Round six Collective commitment—We will create and use common assessments to respond to student needs.		
Round seven Schoolwide goal—Each grade level in our school will prepare students for the next grade level.		
Round eight Schoolwide goal—We will improve student outcomes in our priority area (reading) on our state assessment, paying particular attention to our target groups of students.		

Plus/Delta: Example Four Pillars Key

If staff use this activity across a site, the facilitator may keep responses to help that staff develop or redesign these critical components for their site.

Example	What Is Positive About This Example (+) and Why	What You Would Change About This Example (Δ) and Why
Round one Mission—Our school mission is to support students so they can learn to the best of their ability.	The mission appears to be student-centered and focuses on learning.	The mission does not appear to have a dedication to high levels of learning for all students. This can be clarified.
Round two Mission—Our school mission is to ensure every student learns at high levels and that we do what it takes to make that happen.	There is a commitment to high levels of learning for every student. In addition, there is a commitment to adult actions.	While this mission statement includes a commitment to high levels of learning, the school will want to spend time to make sure they are clear about what adult actions will make that happen.
Round three Vision—Our school vision is to be a place where students want to learn and achieve their goals.	Learning and achieving goals are the focus of the vision. There also appears to be a vision that students will establish their own goals.	It appears a commitment to learning for all students and adults doing what it takes to make that happen is missing from this vision. This should be modified.
Round four Vision—Our school vision is to be a collaborative learning community that meets the needs of every student, resulting in high levels of learning.	There appears to be a commitment to adult collaboration and high levels of learning for all students.	A vision is to be a compelling future. It is possible that this vision could be worded in such a way that provides a bit more inspiration for the future of the school.

Round five Collective commitment—We will work together to achieve school goals.	There is a commitment to having goals and to adults working together.	Adults working together doesn't necessarily mean effective collaboration, and establishing goals doesn't mean they will be based on high levels of learning. Clarification could help.
Round six Collective commitment—We will create and use common assessments to respond to student needs.	There is a commitment to common assessments and using those to support students.	The "we" could be clarified to mention collaborative teams. In addition, the response could be clarified to include interventions and extensions.
Round seven Schoolwide goal—Each grade level in our school will prepare students for the next grade level.	The goal includes every grade level in the building, supporting a collective effort.	When it comes to writing an annual SMART goal, this would be hard to quantify and would be too general. Adding clarity would be beneficial.
Round eight: Schoolwide goal—We will improve student outcomes in our priority area (reading) on our state assessment, paying particular attention to our target groups of students.	This goal provides a priority area and also notes that target groups of students, presumably ones the school has not supported enough in the past, will be a focus. This can easily be turned into an annual SMART* goal.	The goal could be adjusted to specifically name the target groups so the PLC is clear on what needs to occur to achieve the goal.

Reference: Conzemius, A. E., & O'Neill, J. (2014). *The handbook for SMART school teams: Revitalizing best practices for collaboration* (2nd ed.). Bloomington, IN: Solution Tree Press.

---

* SMART: strategic and specific, measurable, attainable, results oriented, and time bound

Doing the Work: Practicing the Four Pillars

My Draft	Why I Wrote My Draft This Way
Mission:	
Vision:	
One collective commitment:	
Goal:	

Chapter Two

Teams

This chapter supports learning about structures and teams within a PLC at Work. Since an entire school or district, rather than an individual team, is understood to be the PLC, it is beneficial for all staff members to understand what school structures look like, even though they may not interact with all the structures daily. This chapter can be thought of as the chapter that takes the concept of a PLC at Work and starts to paint the picture of what it actually looks like in practice.

Understanding Team Structures in a PLC at Work

In the pursuit of excellence for every student, structures, teams, and a move to action are at the heart of a PLC's three big ideas—(1) a focus on learning, (2) a collaborative culture and collective responsibility, and (3) a results orientation (DuFour et al., 2024). While the number of teams and their precise makeup varies from PLC to PLC, most commonly, there is a guiding coalition, schoolwide behavior team, site intervention team, and teacher collaborative teams. People in the school may serve on multiple teams; so, for example, a classroom teacher may serve on the guiding coalition, and a reading specialist may serve on the school intervention team. This is in addition to the regular critical work they engage in with their collaborative team.

Regardless of their makeup or purpose, all teams address the four critical questions of a PLC:

1. What knowledge, skills, and dispositions should every student acquire as a result of this unit, this course, or this grade level?
2. How will we know when each student has acquired the essential knowledge and skills?
3. How will we respond when some students do not learn?
4. How will we extend the learning for students who are already proficient? (DuFour et al., 2024, p. 44)

The following sections address the most common team structures in a PLC.

Guiding Coalition

Because a principal or other identified school leader cannot make every decision necessary to make these three big ideas a reality in the school, a guiding coalition is created to support the school. This team works together to develop a strong understanding of what it takes for an organization to be a PLC and plans for this to become a reality (DuFour et al., 2024). If used appropriately, this team is incredibly impactful. The site's titled leader builds the coalition, ensuring it is made up of those who are willing to live the mission, pursue the vision, stand by the collective commitments, and achieve the goals.

As progress toward becoming a high functioning school becomes a reality, the guiding coalition becomes a defender of the process. However, the guiding coalition's focus is not simply to plan a budget or provide the principal feedback on school operations. The focus is on ensuring the school procedures are set up to foster a PLC, educators have the understanding to implement the processes required in a PLC, and progress is measured toward becoming a PLC. This team operates under the three big ideas as it does the following.

- Ensures learning is the focus of the school
- Acts as a model of collaboration toward common goals
- Measures progress in order to ensure the system is consistently making gains

For some schools, this team may double as the school's leadership team.

Schoolwide Behavior Team

While we strive for academic success for all, behavioral success is a critical component of academic success. A schoolwide behavior team that focuses on schoolwide expected behaviors (Hannigan et al., 2021) is likely to support the PLC process if it is focused, as other teams are, on the four critical questions.

1. What are the essential behaviors all students should display?
2. How will we know if they are displaying these behaviors?
3. How will we intervene if we do not see these behaviors universally?
4. How will we elevate expectations if we are already seeing the expected behaviors across our site?

For example, the team may establish a behavioral matrix for the school (which aligns to critical question one). This team then determines what data they will monitor to determine whether students are meeting those expectations (which aligns to critical question two). If data demonstrate a schoolwide performance gap between behaviors and expectations, the team reteaches the associated expectations. When the site is generally meeting all expectations or improves in the needed area, expectations are either elevated or are celebrated.

Be aware that the schoolwide behavior team is not an intervention team; the former focuses on the Tier 1 instruction for all students. The site intervention team focuses on both academic and behavioral interventions that go beyond the all-student, Tier 1 level. The site leader carefully considers who at the site has the appropriate beliefs, skills, and perspectives when putting together this team.

Site Intervention Team

A school or site intervention team supports the PLC process. This team focuses on the use of schoolwide resources to address universal skills that students may lack or address needs for students who may require focused advanced learning opportunities, including tiered responses to intervention and extensions (Mattos et al., 2024). They generally follow these steps on a regular and ongoing basis.

1. The team first works to understand what students need to be able to perform for proficiency at or above grade level (which responds to critical question one). This team is identifying the critical skills students will need to be successful in a grade level's guaranteed and viable curriculum. For example, students need number sense for success in upper-elementary mathematics.

2. They use universal screening and other available data to determine which students may need interventions on universal skills so they can move toward grade-level expectations. In addition, the team analyzes the same data to determine who could benefit from a focused advanced learning plan based on their grade-level proficiency (to answer critical question two).

3. They determine appropriate interventions and advanced learning opportunities for these students (to answer critical questions three and four). They monitor these data regularly—at least monthly—to ensure the school's resources are being used in the best possible service of students.

It is important to note that this site intervention team does not manage all interventions. The focus is on universal skill interventions that go beyond a grade-level or content area teachers' expertise and are, thus, coordinated using schoolwide resources. Universal skills include reading skills, essential writing skills, number sense, and an understanding of mathematical operations. Interventions for students needing support on standards for their grade level are served by the grade-level or content area teachers.

Teacher Collaborative Team

The most fundamental team is the teacher collaborative team (DuFour et al., 2024), often referred to as *professional learning teams*. Each staff member serves on a team that is oriented to the same goal. Most often, this is a team of educators who teach the same classes or grade level. For example, this would be the team of high school world history teachers or elementary third-grade teachers. When there are not like counterparts in the school or district (a single art teacher at a school, for example), sensible teams are created. These may be grade banded, departmental, or cross-content teams united by common skill-based goals.

When teacher collaborative teams meet, contributing to the PLC, they work to be very specific about what standards and other important skills they expect students to learn in an effort to maximize student growth and achievement. They work to ensure they can accurately measure learning through frequent meaningful assessments. They work to intervene when students have not met learning goals and extend when they have shown proficiency.

This continuous improvement cycle, adopting action research principles, is the core of this team. While it may develop lesson plans together or cooperate in planning other logistics, a true teacher collaborative team focuses time on the four critical questions. In addition, it establishes a yearlong SMART goal aligned with school goals to provide direction. A SMART goal is strategic and specific, measurable, attainable, results oriented, and time bound (Conzemius & O'Neill, 2014).

> ## Discussion Questions and Next Steps Resources
>
> **Consider these questions after reading this chapter.**
>
> * What is your team's common goal? What do you do when not everyone acts in accordance with the team's common goal?
> * Are there people left out of the collaborative team processes who should be included?
> * How can you contribute to making sure your team is focused on the most important work of a team?
>
> Suggested resources follow that can help you take next steps (if your existing PLC has not yet addressed those elements). These are in addition to the foundational texts mentioned in the introduction.
>
> * Michael D. Bayewitz and colleagues' (2020) *Help Your Team: Overcoming Common Collaborative Challenges in a PLC at Work*
> * Anne E. Conzemius and Jan O'Neill's (2014) *The Handbook for SMART School Teams: Revitalizing Best Practices for Collaboration, Second Edition*
> * Bill Hall's (2022) *Powerful Guiding Coalitions: How to Build and Sustain the Leadership Team in Your PLC at Work*
> * Brig Leane and Jon Yost's (2022) *Singletons in a PLC at Work: Navigating On-Ramps to Meaningful Collaboration*
> * Jeanne Spiller and Karen Power's (2019) *Leading With Intention: Eight Areas for Reflection and Planning in Your PLC at Work*

what may come next for them. To complete this tool, you may need to ask questions of your team and school leadership.

The following activities deepen a participant's understanding of teams' structures and roles. As the facilitator, you may choose to use one, some, or all of these learning opportunities based on need. In addition, you can modify any activity to meet adult learners' needs and facilitate engaged learning.

- **Scenarios: Teams** helps participants think about what it really looks like to have PLC at Work structures in place. Participants read a scenario and determine what about it represents PLC structures and what does not. Each scenario allows participants to reasonably complete the entire graphic organizer. The facilitator can easily modify this activity to be done off paper, with only small-group discussion. The facilitator can also modify the scenarios to fit the site or audience more specifically, increasing the relevance.

- **Matching: Responsibilities and Teams** helps participants develop an understanding of which roles belong to which teams. Participants read a team responsibility and indicate which team the responsibility best fits. Answer options include the guiding coalition, schoolwide behavior team, site intervention team, and teacher collaborative team. The facilitator, if alternative names are used at the district or site, can modify the titles appropriately. No matter the delivery method, the facilitator should have time to read individual responses and use that information to correct misconceptions.

- **Doing the Work: Writing Team Roles** deepens understanding of school structures in a PLC by having participants describe each team's role in their own words. While this would not normally be done independently, this activity is intended to develop understanding and confidence. Participants record their understanding of the role of each team in a PLC at Work and

Activities

Before moving on to the activities, ask participants to complete the reproducible "Topic Processing: Teams" (page 32) to ensure they have a foundational understanding that allows them to apply their learning. Then have participants complete the reproducible "Analyzing the Current Reality: Teams" (page 33). It will help you learn the team's understanding of structures and roles and determine then record additions or corrections based on conversation. Facilitators, especially for larger audiences, should check in regularly with discussion groups to help correct misconceptions.

> ### Facilitating Professional Learning
>
> **Connect the learning to participant roles and the school focus.**
>
> Random acts of professional learning, in my experience, will be seen as additive to participants. If the facilitator directly connects how the learning can positively impact participants and aligns with the school's current focus areas, participants will view the learning much more positively, and their motivation to learn will increase (Johansen, Eliassen, & Jeno, 2023). A "self-transcendent purpose," such as improving students' lives, also deepens learning (Yeager et al., 2014). This does not mean that the session needs to be a sales pitch. Rather, it means that the session needs to be explicitly relevant to participants.

Scenarios: Teams

In this activity, participants review scenarios to discuss and identify what parts of each scenario are representative of PLC at Work structures and what parts are not. While some of the scenarios may seem obvious, discussing *why* makes this learning activity meaningful.

Follow these steps.

1. Before beginning, ensure some type of professional learning was shared to support the participants' understanding. This may be reading and debriefing this chapter's text.

2. Provide each participant with a copy of "Scenarios: Teams" (page 34) or display for all to read. Keep a copy of "Scenarios: Teams Key" (page 36) for yourself to support discussion.

3. Ensure each participant has a partner or group to engage with. Cap groups at four people to allow effective discussion.

4. One round at a time, have participants read a scenario. Participants then, in the What Is Representative of a PLC and What Is *Not* Representative of a PLC columns, record details from the scenarios accordingly. Ask participants to refrain from moving on to the next round when they are done.

5. After each participant has read the scenario and recorded their rationale, they discuss it with their partner or group. This can include the facilitator checking for consensus on their rationale and engaging in conversation where there may be disagreement. For example, the facilitator may ask for participants to share their answer, the rationale for their answer, and doubts about their answer.

6. If there is more than one group of participants, facilitate a whole-group conversation to see if there is consensus or dissonance on the rationale.

7. Pending the group's answers, further discussion may be needed to provide a deeper understanding of the suggested answers and evidence. For example, if there are significant disagreements or misunderstandings, the facilitator may need to refer to resources on the concept to provide participants additional opportunities to learn.

8. Provide the group with the suggested answers from "Scenarios: Teams Key" to spur further conversation.

9. Proceed to the subsequent rounds, repeating the process.

Matching: Responsibilities and Teams

In this activity, participants review team responsibilities. For each responsibility listed, participants match the appropriate team. As with most sample activities, it is the discussion of *why* that makes this learning activity meaningful.

Follow these steps.

1. Before beginning, ensure that some type of professional learning was shared to support the participants' understanding. This may be reading and debriefing this chapter's text.

2. Provide each participant with a copy of "Matching: Responsibilities and Teams" (page 38) or display for all to read. Keep a copy of "Matching: Responsibilities and Teams Key" (page 39) for yourself to support discussion.

3. Ensure that each participant has a partner or group to engage with. Cap groups at four people to allow effective discussion.

4. For each responsibility listed in the that column, participants should select the appropriate team in the Which Team This Responsibility Fits Best column. All teams will be selected at least once, and some will be selected more than once. They should also record their rationale for choosing the team (or not choosing the other teams).

5. After each participant has finished, they discuss with their partner or group.

6. If there is more than one group of participants, facilitate a whole-group conversation to see if there is consensus or dissonance on the rationale.

7. Provide the group with the answers from "Matching: Responsibilities and Teams Key" to spur further conversation.

8. Pending the group's answers, further discussion may be needed to provide a deeper understanding of the suggested answers and evidence. For example, if there are significant disagreements or misunderstandings, the facilitator may need to refer to resources on the concept to provide participants additional opportunities to learn.

9. Proceed to the second and subsequent rounds, repeating the process.

Doing the Work: Writing Team Roles

In this activity, participants review team roles in a PLC at Work. For each team, participants record their understanding of the team's role. In addition, they engage in dialogue to refine their thinking. This dialogue allows them greater understanding through processing learned information.

Follow these steps.

1. Before beginning, ensure that some type of professional learning was shared to support the participants' understanding. This may be reading and debriefing this chapter's text.

2. Provide each participant with a copy of "Doing the Work: Writing Team Roles" (page 40) or display for all to read. Keep a copy of "Doing the Work: Writing Team Roles Key" (page 41) for yourself to support discussion.

3. Ensure each participant has a partner or group to engage with. Cap groups at four people to allow effective discussion.

4. For each team listed in the My Understanding of the Team Role column, participants write what they believe that team does. Another way to phrase the prompt is to ask, "What is this team's purpose?"

5. After each participant has finished, they discuss their response with their partner or group.
6. If there is more than one group of participants, facilitate a whole-group conversation to see if there is consensus or dissonance on the rationale.
7. Provide the group with the answers from "Doing the Work: Writing Team Roles Key" to spur further conversation.
8. Pending the group's answers, further discussion may be needed to provide a deeper understanding of the suggested answers and evidence. For example, if there are significant disagreements or misunderstandings, the facilitator may need to refer to resources on the concept to provide participants additional opportunities to learn.
9. Proceed to the second and subsequent rounds, repeating the process.

Topic Processing: Teams

Based on reflection, what are current successes and current growth areas for me, my team, or my school, and why?	What are my next actions to grow in my understanding?	Where can I get support to grow?

Analyzing the Current Reality: Teams

To complete this tool, you may need to ask questions of your team and school leadership. Doing so will assist your understanding and help you learn what may come next for your team. The evidence column allows you to provide specific evidence of the current reality.

Structure	Current Reality	Evidence
The school has a guiding coalition that serves to support the PLC process.	☐ Not at all true. ☐ Somewhat true. ☐ Mostly true. ☐ Always true.	
The school has a team that establishes behavioral expectations, ensures these are taught, and monitors needs on an ongoing basis.	☐ Not at all true. ☐ Somewhat true. ☐ Mostly true. ☐ Always true.	
The school has a site intervention team that utilizes schoolwide resources to meet student academic and behavioral needs that go beyond the expertise of the collaborative team.	☐ Not at all true. ☐ Somewhat true. ☐ Mostly true. ☐ Always true.	
Each certified staff member serves on a collaborative team and focuses on the four critical questions of a PLC.	☐ Not at all true. ☐ Somewhat true. ☐ Mostly true. ☐ Always true.	

Propel Your PLC at Work © 2025 Solution Tree Press • SolutionTree.com
Visit **go.SolutionTree.com/PLCbooks** to download this free reproducible.

Scenarios: Teams

Scenario	What Is Representative of a PLC	What Is Not Representative of a PLC
Round one A school principal establishes a guiding coalition of staff willing to learn and support other adults across the school site. The agendas of this team include reviewing assessment schedules, planning family engagement activities, and determining how to spend school funds on supplies.		
Round two A school establishes a guiding coalition. This team has collaboratively developed a mission statement that focuses the team on supporting the school as a whole in becoming a PLC. This includes learning about the best ways to solve school concerns and supporting the school based on that learning.		
Round three A school has a schoolwide behavior team that meets quarterly. This team, based on representation from the school, establishes behavioral expectations for students, plans how to deliberately teach these expectations, and monitors schoolwide behaviors monthly. As a result of this monitoring, actions are taken to address areas of concern.		

page 1 of 2

Propel Your PLC at Work © 2025 Solution Tree Press • SolutionTree.com
Visit **go.SolutionTree.com/PLCbooks** to download this free reproducible.

Round four A site intervention team is established to plan and monitor interventions. This team of specialists meets in the fall to plan who is going to be in what intervention. In the spring, the team reconvenes to determine whether students were well served in each intervention.		
Round five Each educator in the school serves on a collaborative team that meets weekly. These teams are focused on determining what learning is most critical, how they will assess that learning, and how they will intervene when students have not met critical learning goals.		

Scenarios: Teams Key

Scenario	What Is Representative of a PLC	What Is Not Representative of a PLC
Round one *A school principal establishes a guiding coalition of staff willing to learn and support other adults across the school site. The agendas of this team include reviewing assessment schedules, planning family engagement activities, and determining how to spend school funds on supplies.*	A school leadership structure exists that can impact adult learning across the school site.	The focus of this team is not on the impactful PLC process. Rather, it is focused on business items that do not, necessarily, move learning forward for students.
Round two *A school establishes a guiding coalition. This team has collaboratively developed a mission statement that focuses the team on supporting the school as a whole in becoming a PLC. This includes learning about the best ways to solve school concerns and supporting the school based on that learning.*	A team is established that focuses on adult learning. Particularly, they are learning about the PLC process and bringing that learning to the staff at large.	While there is a clear goal for this team, the scenario does not share how they are working collaboratively with the entire staff to move the work forward. This may be a discussion point for this team.
Round three *A school has a schoolwide behavior team that meets quarterly. This team, based on representation from the school, establishes behavioral expectations for students, plans how to deliberately teach these expectations, and monitors schoolwide behaviors monthly. As a result of this monitoring, actions are taken to address areas of concern.*	The school has established a schoolwide behavior team that establishes expectations, plans to teach them, monitors success, and plans to address needs. There is also representation from various school staff.	The team meets only quarterly. The team likely needs to meet more frequently in order to successfully fulfill their role. Any team focused on the four critical questions will have limited success meeting only four times per year.

Round four A site intervention team is established to plan and monitor interventions. This team of specialists meets in the fall to plan who is going to be in what intervention. In the spring, the team reconvenes to determine whether students were well served in each intervention.	The scenario shows the school has established a team and has implemented a series of interventions. It also appears there is an expectation of learning in the interventions based on the end-of-year monitoring.	This team meets far too infrequently to effectively monitor and adjust. Students in need could be missing their opportunity for intervention, and those ready to exit do not have the opportunity to do so until the next school year.
Round five Each educator in the school serves on a collaborative team that meets weekly. These teams are focused on determining what learning is most critical, how they will assess that learning, and how they will intervene when students have not met critical learning goals.	Each member of the school community serves on a team, and the focus for each team is on results.	It is unclear if these teams also look at modifying adult practices and at extension opportunities for students. These are also a part of the PLC process.

Matching: Responsibilities and Teams

Responsibility	Which Team This Responsibility Fits Best and Why
Round one This team uses the four critical questions of a PLC to support students who may need to develop universal skills that go beyond the general expertise of a grade level or content teacher.	☐ Guiding coalition ☐ Schoolwide behavior team ☐ Site intervention team ☐ Teacher collaborative team
Round two This team focuses on student expectations for how they conduct themselves as students. The team utilizes the four critical questions of a PLC to support this work.	☐ Guiding coalition ☐ Schoolwide behavior team ☐ Site intervention team ☐ Teacher collaborative team
Round three This team works to support the whole school in developing a strong understanding of what it takes for the site to become a PLC.	☐ Guiding coalition ☐ Schoolwide behavior team ☐ Site intervention team ☐ Teacher collaborative team
Round four This team meets to support student academic learning on identified essential standards or other essential learning. They use common assessments, analyze those assessments, and intervene or extend based on those assessments.	☐ Guiding coalition ☐ Schoolwide behavior team ☐ Site intervention team ☐ Teacher collaborative team
Round five This team may double as the school's leadership team but goes well beyond traditional leadership team actions that reflect school management or provide feedback to a principal.	☐ Guiding coalition ☐ Schoolwide behavior team ☐ Site intervention team ☐ Teacher collaborative team
Round six This team is often made up of educators who teach the same course, content area, or have another logical link to each other.	☐ Guiding coalition ☐ Schoolwide behavior team ☐ Site intervention team ☐ Teacher collaborative team

Propel Your PLC at Work © 2025 Solution Tree Press • SolutionTree.com
Visit **go.SolutionTree.com/PLCbooks** to download this free reproducible.

Matching: Responsibilities and Teams Key

Responsibility	Which Teams This Responsibility Fits Best and Why
Round one This team uses the four critical questions of a PLC to support students who may need to develop universal skills that go beyond the general expertise of a grade level or content teacher.	☐ Guiding coalition ☐ Schoolwide behavior team ☑ Site intervention team ☐ Teacher collaborative team
Round two This team focuses on student expectations for how they conduct themselves as students. The team utilizes the four critical questions of a PLC to support this work.	☐ Guiding coalition ☑ Schoolwide behavior team ☐ Site intervention team ☐ Teacher collaborative team
Round three This team works to support the whole school in developing a strong understanding of what it takes for the site to become a PLC.	☑ Guiding coalition ☐ Schoolwide behavior team ☐ Site intervention team ☐ Teacher collaborative team
Round four This team meets to support student academic learning on identified essential standards or other essential learning. They use common assessments, analyze those assessments, and intervene or extend based on those assessments.	☐ Guiding coalition ☐ Schoolwide behavior team ☐ Site intervention team ☑ Teacher collaborative team
Round five This team may double as the school's leadership team but goes well beyond traditional leadership team actions that reflect school management or provide feedback to a principal.	☑ Guiding coalition ☐ Schoolwide behavior team ☐ Site intervention team ☐ Teacher collaborative team
Round six This team is often made up of educators who teach the same course, content area, or have another logical link to each other.	☐ Guiding coalition ☐ Schoolwide behavior team ☐ Site intervention team ☑ Teacher collaborative team

Propel Your PLC at Work © 2025 Solution Tree Press • SolutionTree.com
Visit **go.SolutionTree.com/PLCbooks** to download this free reproducible.

Doing the Work: Writing Team Roles

My Understanding of the Team Role and Why	Additions or Corrections Based on Conversation
Guiding coalition:	
Schoolwide behavior team:	
Site intervention team:	
Teacher collaborative team:	

Doing the Work: Writing Team Roles Key

My Understanding of the Team Role and Why	Additions or Corrections Based on Conversation
Guiding coalition: This team's role is to gain a deep understanding of the PLC at Work process and provide ongoing support for the PLC process at their site (DuFour et al., 2024).	
Schoolwide behavior team: This team's role is to determine schoolwide behavioral expectations and plan for deliberately teaching those expectations. In addition, this team monitors how students are doing with meeting expectations, implementing plans to celebrate and address needs (Hannigan et al., 2021).	
Site intervention team: This team's role is to support students by identifying needs for intensive interventions, implementing those interventions, and monitoring those interventions (Mattos et al., 2024).	
Teacher collaborative team: This team's role is to work collaboratively, using the four critical questions of a PLC, to obtain high levels of learning for every student (DuFour et al., 2024).	

References

Mattos, M., Buffum, A., & Malone, J., Cruz, L. F., Dimich, N., & Schuhl, S. (2024). *Taking action: A handbook for RTI at Work* (2nd ed.). Bloomington, IN: Solution Tree Press.

DuFour, R., DuFour, R., Eaker, R., Many, T. W., Mattos, M., & Muhammad, A. (2024). *Learning by doing: A handbook for Professional Learning Communities at Work* (4th ed.). Bloomington, IN: Solution Tree Press.

Chapter Three

Collaborative Teams

The previous chapter focused on sharing the roles and responsibilities of the various teams that support the PLC at Work process. This chapter zooms in to provide more information on the collaborative teacher teams, which are the most frequent team found in the process. Collaborative teams are united by common goals and a unit-by-unit process for improving learning outcomes. Human nature, however, requires agreements and processes to ensure teams function at high levels because our individual behaviors are not always conducive to working effectively in teams. Teams must get after the work by focusing on the regular tasks of the teaching-assessing-learning cycle, but time must also be carved out to discuss and monitor how the team is functioning. This is time worth spending if reflection occurs that results in the team refining its processes moving forward. It improves the team's effectiveness.

Understanding the Collaborative Team's Role

Collaborative teams are the integral element of a school functioning as a PLC. While the other elements of the process are important, it all comes together only when collaborative teams function at high levels by following processes that embody the three big ideas—a focus on learning, collaboration, and a results orientation. These teams of educators may teach the same courses, focus on similar skills, or serve students in a similar way. You may, for example, serve on a team with other third-grade teachers, with other educators focusing on disciplinary literacy, or with fellow counselors who monitor and support social-emotional learning. Regardless, the focus is the same. Collaborative teams use an ongoing improvement process—including applying the teaching-assessing-learning cycle—to achieve their goals, contributing to the PLC as a whole. This text provides an overview of how a collaborative team functions. The teams' goals, how they intersect with the four critical questions and the cycle, and considerations for team success are all covered. The teaching-assessing-learning cycle as a whole is covered in chapter 8 (page 133).

Note that this section is written in the context of a collaborative team formed around teachers who share a common course or content. However, that is only a percentage of teams. Vertically and across disciplines, teams apply the same principles to the learning they are emphasizing as a team. This chapter does not focus on other teams that support the PLC at Work process.

Team Goal

Collaborative teams, as they are united by a common purpose, set an annual goal as a team to focus on that purpose (DuFour et al., 2024). That goal is typically written in one of the following formats.

1. FAST (frequently discussed, ambitious, specific, and transparent; Drucker, 1954)
2. SMART (specific, measurable, achievable, realistic, and time bound; Conzemius & O'Neill, 2014)

In many cases, teams write goals based on historical data, addressing an area of need. For example, this goal may include increasing reading comprehension through teachers studying the topic and implementing new practices. Teams may also write goals, particularly during early years of implementation, that focus on using the teaching-assessing-learning cycle to impact learning. For example, this may include setting a goal for at least 80 percent of students meeting proficiency in each cycle and 95 percent achieving proficiency in each cycle after an opportunity for interventions. After implementation, this type of goal becomes inherent to the process.

However, before the team collaborates and agrees on that goal, they comprehensively analyze relevant data to determine where the team needs to enhance their adult practice to more strongly impact student learning or focus their efforts to achieve high levels of learning. This can include state assessment data, local screening data, and classroom data, which can inform specific areas of need. For maximum effectiveness at the school, the team's goal aligns to the larger goals established by the site. No matter what data they use to set a goal and how they write it, teams monitor their progress toward this goal on a regular basis. Usually, this monitoring occurs monthly or unit by unit.

While the goal is important, the real magic is in the action plans the team outlines to reach the goal. For example, a team can pledge to increase proficiency in reading, in numeracy, or in unit proficiency. However, establishing a goal in and of itself does not mean any adult behavior will change. Actions determine who will do what by when toward the goal. The team establishes a plan to learn together to enhance their practice. This process takes an annual goal and turns it into impact for the team's educators.

The Four Critical Questions and the Teaching-Assessing-Learning Cycle

The goal the team establishes provides a yearlong focus for learning and addresses instructional and student needs. However, there is much more that unites the team than this single goal. The team is focused on their impact on learning. This goes back to the three big ideas of a PLC: (1) a focus on learning, (2) a collaborative culture, and (3) a focus on results (DuFour et al., 2024).

For the team to effectively focus on the three big ideas, they operate under four critical questions (page 8). Each of these questions has its own intricacies. The summaries, however, follow.

- To answer, "What knowledge, skills, and dispositions should every student acquire as a result of this unit, this course, or this grade level?" (DuFour et al., 2024, p. 44), prioritize what is most valuable for students to learn as we can't teach, measure learning, and intervene or extend every educational standard for which we are responsible.
- To answer, "How will we know when each student has acquired the essential knowledge

and skills?" (DuFour et al., 2024, p. 44), design quality assessments that reveal data by standard or target to inform instruction and provide quality feedback to students.

- To answer, "How will we respond when some students do not learn?" (DuFour et al., 2024), focus on structures and action plans for students who do not meet the goals set out on critical question one as determined by the assessments for critical question two.

- To answer, "How will we extend the learning for students who are already proficient?" (DuFour et al., 2024, p. 44), use the same data to determine which students need alternative opportunities based on current skill successes.

The four critical questions of a PLC may seem simple. However, they are more complex than they may appear at first glance. Particularly, critical question one requires time and processes the other questions hinge on. This includes determining essential standards for each course students have the opportunity to take, which impacts the curricula.

Due to their complexities, a system must be in place for teams to effectively use the questions in an ongoing process. That system of ongoing learning and continuous improvement is the teaching-assessing-learning cycle. In this cycle, collaborative teams engage in a unit-by-unit process. Essentially, the team takes the following steps.

1. The team determines the unit focus by determining learning targets (which addresses critical question one).
2. The team agrees on assessments to check on progress of learning (which addresses critical question two).
3. The team analyzes the agreed-on completed assessments to determine interventions for students demonstrating struggle and differentiation for learners demonstrating success (which addresses critical questions three and four).
4. The team uses that data to immediately revise their instruction to try to meet student needs (and the data also inform instruction in later units).

As an example, assume three teachers are going to teach a unit on multiplying fractions. They first determine the unit's essential learning targets, specifically looking at any essential standards they have determined to be related to the unit. They then plan the end-of-unit assessment and interim assessments (checkpoints) that will prove useful for monitoring learning throughout the unit. While teachers assess more frequently in their own classroom, teachers on teams collaboratively analyze common assessments to determine their next steps for supporting instruction and students.

Considerations for Team Success

Teams establishing an annual goal, pursuing that goal, and operating under a unit-by-unit teaching-assessing-learning cycle may seem simple enough. However, human nature and differing opinions of professional educators can make the work more complex. Professionals embracing the process, as compared to those simply doing a job, establish certain systems and use practices that ensure the team functions at a high level.

Outside the focus on the goal and the cycle, the team has the following musts.

- **The team must establish norms (working agreements) to ensure that all members know what behaviors are expected (DuFour et al., 2024):** Collaboratively establishing these norms will build clarity and permission for the team to hold each other accountable to the established behaviors.

- **The team must be clear about what the meeting's focus is:** This means there must be a meeting agenda or a standing process. Each member must see that the meeting time is valued and understand what they need to do to prepare for the meeting.

- **The team must practice and embrace data sharing:** A team can assemble and agree on the focus of the learning and how they will assess students rather easily in comparison to the vulnerability needed to share results of the assessments with team peers. Many teams simply meet and loosely discuss student performance. Teams open to vulnerability are not worried about what colleagues will think of them and, therefore, share their classroom data and seek and share ideas for improving the team's instruction. However, without analyzing data, the team can't address students' instructional needs. In that case, the meeting has minimal to no benefit. It behooves the team to openly discuss vulnerability, as well as receive coaching for it and practice it, so members can begin trusting each other.

- **The team must discuss and learn to embrace dissonance:** This embrace comes with trust, just as openly sharing data does. A team that does not discuss instructional practice and constructively push each other will likely keep using the same practices and processes regardless of what data show. Teams that healthily discuss the merits of several ideas without attacking the proposing individual stand a stronger chance to be innovative and advance their practice to ultimately benefit students (Satterstrom, Kerrissey, & DiBenigno, 2022).

- **The team must embrace professionalism:** While this connects the previous considerations, it is worth mentioning on its own. The education profession exists to benefit each and every student. This will not happen by treating teaching as a job. Educators must understand that reflecting, staying informed about best practices, collaborating, and taking informed risk are all part of what makes a professional educator. In team meetings, there is a stark difference between educators showing up to their team meetings as professionals and educators showing up out of compliance. As shared by teacher and author Hal Urban (2003), "Attitude is a choice, maybe the most important one you will ever make" (p. 47).

Discussion Questions and Next Steps Resources

Consider these questions after reading this chapter.

* How does your team establish and monitor their goals?
* What processes are in place to ensure the team focuses on the four critical questions of a PLC?
* Is the team at a stage where members are engaged in learning together, or are action steps needed to achieve this level of team performance?

Suggested resources follow that can help you take next steps (if your existing PLC has not yet addressed those elements). These are in addition to the foundational texts mentioned in the introduction.

* Kim Bailey and Chris Jakicic's (2019) *Make It Happen*
* Kim Bailey and Chris Jakicic's (2023) *Common Formative Assessment: A Toolkit for Professional Learning Communities at Work*, Second Edition
* Michael D. Bayewitz and colleagues' (2020) *Help Your Team*
* William M. Ferriter's (2020) *The Big Book of Tools for Collaborative Teams in a PLC at Work*
* William M. Ferriter, Mike Mattos, and Rob J. Meyer's (2025) *The Big Book of Tools for RTI at Work*
* Colin Sloper and Gavin Grift's (2021) *Collaborative Teams That Work: The Definitive Guide to Cycles of Learning in a PLC*

Activities

Before moving on to the three activities, ask participants to complete the reproducible "Topic Processing: Collaborative Teams" (page 50) to ensure they have a foundational understanding that allows them to apply their learning. Then have participants complete the reproducible "Analyzing the Current Reality: Collaborative Teams" (page 51). It will help you understand the team's understanding of that team type's role and determine what may come next for them. To complete this tool, you may need to ask questions of your team and school leadership.

The following activities deepen a participant's understanding of collaborative teams' (usually made up of teachers) structures and roles. As the facilitator, you may choose to use one, some, or all of these learning opportunities based on need. In addition, you can modify any activity to meet adult learners' needs and facilitate engaged learning.

- **Scenarios: Collaborative Team** helps participants differentiate between what makes a PLC's collaborative team effective and what does not. In this activity, participants contemplate collaborative team scenarios and complete a graphic organizer. This graphic organizer asks them to analyze the quote provided as the scenario and determine what about that quote is representative of a collaborative team in a PLC at Work and what is not representative of a collaborative team in a PLC at Work. Each of the scenario quotes provided has both elements. A great way for a facilitator to increase engagement in this activity is to have a person or small group act out the scenarios.

- **Ranking: Effective Teams** helps deepen understanding of what makes an effective collaborative team. In this activity, participants read five descriptions of collaborative teams and then use their knowledge to rank the teams by effectiveness level. In addition, the provided graphic organizer allows participants to record their rationale. It is suggested the facilitator emphasizes the discussion of ranking rationale in the process to enrich the learning.

- **Doing the Work: Critical Considerations of a Collaborative Team** is intended to deepen the understanding of collaborative teams by having participants process how they would suggest their team address key considerations. This is normally addressed by the team as a whole, but this activity provides an opportunity for individuals to process learning and envision what a team may look like in operation. The provided graphic organizer can also be easily adapted for collaborative teams to record their process.

Facilitating Professional Learning

Start with building connections.

The professional learning session's facilitator may or may not have developed relationships with participants. Even if relationships exist, the facilitator should take time for the team to develop connections. While ten minutes is desirable, even three to five minutes is beneficial. Quality professional learning sessions involve deep discussion, thinking, and vulnerability. It is difficult for participants to fully engage that way without warming up. Providing an opportunity for participants to learn about each other, share their thinking, or separate themselves from events earlier in the day at the onset of the learning session will pay off.

Scenarios: Collaborative Teams

In this activity, participants review scenarios to discuss and identify what parts of the scenario represent the role of a collaborative team in a PLC at Work and what parts do not. While some of the scenarios may seem obvious, it is the discussion of *why* that makes this learning activity meaningful.

Follow these steps.

1. Before beginning, ensure some type of professional learning was shared to support the participants' understanding.

This may be reading and debriefing this chapter's text.

2. Provide each participant with a copy of "Scenarios: Collaborative Teams" (page 52) or display for all to read. Keep a copy of "Scenarios: Collaborative Teams Key" (page 54) for yourself to support discussion.

3. Ensure each participant has a partner or group to engage with. Cap groups at four people to allow effective discussion.

4. One round at a time, have participants read a scenario. Participants then, in the What Is Representative of a PLC and What Is *Not* Representative of a PLC columns, record details from the scenarios accordingly. Ask participants to refrain from moving on to the next round when they are done.

5. After each participant has read the scenario and recorded their rationale, they discuss with their partner or group. This can include the facilitator checking for consensus on their rationale and engaging in conversation where there may be disagreement. For example, the facilitator may ask for participants to share their answer, the rationale for their answer, and doubts about their answer.

6. If there is more than one group of participants, facilitate a whole-group conversation to see if there is consensus or dissonance on the rationale.

7. Provide the group with the answers from "Scenarios: Collaborative Teams Key" to spur further conversation.

8. Pending the group's answers, further discussion may be needed to provide a deeper understanding of the suggested answers and evidence. For example, if there are significant disagreements or misunderstandings, the facilitator may need to refer to resources on the concept to provide participants additional opportunities to learn.

9. Proceed to subsequent rounds, repeating the process.

Ranking: Effective Teams

In this activity, participants review team descriptions and rank those teams in order of most to least effective. This activity allows for individual thinking as well as collaboration to develop an understanding of what makes teams effective.

Follow these steps.

1. Before beginning, ensure that some type of professional learning was shared to support the participants' understanding. This may be reading and debriefing this chapter's text.

2. Provide each participant with a copy of "Ranking: Effective Teams" (page 56) or display for all to read. Keep a copy of "Ranking: Effective Teams Key" (page 57) for yourself to support discussion.

3. Ensure each participant has a partner or group to engage with. Cap groups at four people to allow effective discussion.

4. Participants read the five team descriptions and then indicate their effectiveness in the Rank column; 1 is the most effective team, and 5 is the least effective. They should use each number one time and explain in the Rationale for Rank column. An alternative is for the facilitator to provide each team description on individual cards, having participants or teams visually rank each scenario.

5. After each participant has read the scenario and recorded their rationale, they discuss it with their partner or group. This can include checking for consensus on their rationale and discussing disagreements.

6. If there is more than one group of participants, facilitate a whole-group conversation to see if there is consensus or dissonance on the rationale.

7. Provide the group with the answers from "Ranking: Effective Teams Key" to spur further conversation. Note that there may be justifiable differences between the example answers and the participants' answers. This can be a great discussion point.

8. Pending the group's answers, further discussion may be needed to provide a deeper understanding of the suggested answers and evidence. For example, if there are significant disagreements or misunderstandings, the facilitator may need to refer to resources on the concept to provide participants additional opportunities to learn.

9. Proceed to subsequent rounds, repeating the process.

Doing the Work: Critical Considerations of a Collaborative Team

In this activity, participants review considerations for collaborative teams. For each consideration listed, participants record how they believe their team can use the consideration. As with most sample activities, it is the discussion that makes this learning activity meaningful.

Follow these steps.

1. Before beginning, ensure some type of professional learning was shared to support the participants' understanding. This may be reading and debriefing this chapter's text.

2. Provide each participant with a copy of "Doing the Work: Critical Considerations of a Collaborative Team" (page 58) or display for all to read. Keep a copy of "Doing the Work: Critical Considerations of a Collaborative Team Key" (page 59) for yourself to support discussion.

3. Ensure each participant has a partner or group to engage with. Cap groups at four people to allow effective discussion.

4. For each entry in the Critical Consideration column, participants record their thoughts in the How I Suggest My Team Address This Consideration column. Another way to phrase the prompt is to ask, "What would this look like for our team?"

5. After each participant has read the scenario and recorded their rationale, they discuss with their partner or group. This can include the facilitator checking for consensus on their rationale and engaging in conversation where there may be disagreement. For example, the facilitator may ask for participants to share their answer, the rationale for their answer, and doubts about their answer.

6. If there is more than one group of participants, facilitate a whole-group conversation to see if there is consensus or dissonance on the rationale.

7. Provide the group with the answers from "Doing the Work: Critical Considerations of a Collaborative Team Key" to spur further conversation. Note that there may be justifiable differences between the example answers and the participants' answers. This can be a great discussion point.

8. Pending the group's answers, further discussion may be needed to provide a deeper understanding of the suggested answers and evidence. For example, if there are significant disagreements or misunderstandings, the facilitator may need to refer to resources on the concept to provide participants additional opportunities to learn.

9. Proceed to subsequent rounds, repeating the process.

Topic Processing: Collaborative Teams

Is this a success area or a growth area for me, my team, or my school, and why?	What are my next steps to grow in my understanding?	Where can I get support to grow?

Propel Your PLC at Work © 2025 Solution Tree Press • SolutionTree.com
Visit **go.SolutionTree.com/PLCbooks** to download this free reproducible.

Analyzing the Current Reality: Collaborative Teams

To complete this tool, you may need to ask questions of your team and school leadership. Doing so will assist your understanding and help you learn what may come next for your team. The evidence column allows you to provide specific evidence of the current reality.

Critical Consideration	Current Reality	Evidence
My team has established norms or working agreements to ensure there are clearly expected behaviors.	☐ Not at all true. ☐ Somewhat true. ☐ Mostly true. ☐ Always true.	
My team has a process to establish the clear focus of each collaborative team meeting.	☐ Not at all true. ☐ Somewhat true. ☐ Mostly true. ☐ Always true.	
My team openly shares data to foster conversations that impact adult practice and help make plans for student needs.	☐ Not at all true. ☐ Somewhat true. ☐ Mostly true. ☐ Always true.	
My team is able to share differing ideas and is open to hearing differing perspectives.	☐ Not at all true. ☐ Somewhat true. ☐ Mostly true. ☐ Always true.	
Members of my team take the work of a collaborative team seriously, leading to greater impacts of the team.	☐ Not at all true. ☐ Somewhat true. ☐ Mostly true. ☐ Always true.	

Propel Your PLC at Work © 2025 Solution Tree Press • SolutionTree.com
Visit **go.SolutionTree.com/PLCbooks** to download this free reproducible.

Scenarios: Collaborative Teams

Scenario	What Is Representative of a PLC	What Is Not Representative of a PLC
Round one At a team meeting, one member states: "I have 75 percent of my students meeting our learning goal from our last unit. I noticed you had 95 percent meeting our learning goal. Could we talk about strategies you used so I can learn? I would really like to help next year's students."		
Round two At a team meeting, one member states: "I don't know what we have planned to talk about today, but I have to grade some papers and get back to some parents. So, if we could hurry this along, I am sure we can talk about our student concerns next week."		
Round three At a team meeting, one member states: "I like the assessments we design. However, I don't have time to do our common assessments. I have a lot of information to share with students, and testing gets in the way of my ability to cover content."		

Round four		
At a team meeting, one member states: "We should be teaching the same things in our classes. That makes sense. The same course means the same learning goals. However, my student performance is my business. I don't need to share data. I just need to take care of my kids."		

Round five		
A principal states: "ELA improvement and math improvement are our school goals. Therefore, we will form collaborative teams for our ELA and math departments."		

Scenarios: Collaborative Teams Key

Scenario	What Is Representative of a PLC	What Is Not Representative of a PLC
Round one At a team meeting, one member states: "I have 75 percent of my students meeting our learning goal from our last unit. I noticed you had 95 percent meeting our learning goal. Could we talk about strategies you used so I can learn? I would really like to help next year's students."	There is sharing of data. In addition, there is vulnerability from a teacher admitting they did not meet the same performance level as a peer and asking for learning support.	While the teacher asked for learning support, they indicated it was for the following year. The teacher should be accountable for learning this year as well as in future years.
Round two At a team meeting, one member states: "I don't know what we have planned to talk about today, but I have to grade some papers and get back to some parents. So, if we could hurry this along, I am sure we can talk about our student concerns next week."	This team appears to have a consistent meeting, and the focus is on students.	This person does not appear to value provided time and prioritizes other work over the work of the team. In addition, the person hints that the team conversations are based on student concerns and not on plans of support, extension, and changes in adult practice.
Round three At a team meeting, one member states: "I like the assessments we design. However, I don't have time to do our common assessments. I have a lot of information to share with students, and testing gets in the way of my ability to cover content."	The person acknowledges the responsibility of the team to design and utilize common assessments.	The person does not understand that learning is more important than the amount of content they are able to cover. The four critical questions of a PLC are about learning, not about content coverage.

Round four At a team meeting, one member states: "We should be teaching the same things in our classes. That makes sense. The same course means the same learning goals. However, my student performance is my business. I don't need to share data. I just need to take care of my kids."	The person understands the importance of a guaranteed curriculum for a course and has a passion for serving their students.	This person does not understand the importance of collaboration, which leads to better adult practice. This person either needs support with being more vulnerable or in trusting colleagues.
Round five A principal states: "ELA improvement and math improvement are our school goals. Therefore, we will form collaborative teams for our ELA and math departments."	This principal appears to have developed school goals and focus areas.	This principal appears to not understand that the whole school must be organized to serve all students and that everyone should serve on a collaborative team based on a common purpose. This statement creates only two teams.

Ranking: Effective Teams

Insert one check mark for each team, A through D, ranking the entirety of those teams 1 through 5. In that ranking, 1 is the most effective team, adhering closest to the PLC at Work concepts, and so on.

Team Description	Rank	Rationale for Rank
Team A This team comes to each established team meeting time and first discusses what they will talk about that day. This usually includes how they will divide lesson plan writing for the next few weeks.	☐ 1 ☐ 2 ☐ 3 ☐ 4 ☐ 5	
Team B This team uses an agenda that focuses on the four critical questions of a PLC each time they meet. When they analyze data, they discuss how they can share the load of addressing student needs. This includes intervention and extension. In addition, they reflect on their instructional strategies and make commitments to improving their practice.	☐ 1 ☐ 2 ☐ 3 ☐ 4 ☐ 5	
Team C This team comes to each meeting already knowing what the focus will be. When this team decides to use a common assessment, they bring necessary data to the next meeting. Based on that assessment data, they discuss strategies they can use in their classrooms to address students in need of extra support.	☐ 1 ☐ 2 ☐ 3 ☐ 4 ☐ 5	
Team D This team meets weekly. The focus of each meeting is determining essential standards, unpacking those standards, and developing common proficiency. This team uses this information to guide their work in individual classrooms.	☐ 1 ☐ 2 ☐ 3 ☐ 4 ☐ 5	
Team E This team only comes to a meeting when they know their supervising administrator will be attending. At those meetings, which occur about once per month, they focus on pacing for an upcoming unit of study.	☐ 1 ☐ 2 ☐ 3 ☐ 4 ☐ 5	

Propel Your PLC at Work © 2025 Solution Tree Press • SolutionTree.com
Visit **go.SolutionTree.com/PLCbooks** to download this free reproducible.

Ranking: Effective Teams Key

Insert one check mark for each team, A through D, ranking the entirety of those teams 1 through 5. In that ranking, 1 is the most effective team, adhering closest to the PLC at Work concepts, and so on.

Team Description	Rank	Example Rationale for Rank
Team A This team comes to each established team meeting time and first discusses what they will talk about that day. This usually includes how they will divide lesson plan writing for the next few weeks.	☐ 1 ☐ 2 ☐ 3 ☑ 4 ☐ 5	This team is ranked fourth, not very effective, as it does not have a shared agenda and does not focus on the four critical questions of a PLC.
Team B This team uses an agenda that focuses on the four critical questions of a PLC each time they meet. When they analyze data, they discuss how they can share the load of addressing student needs. This includes intervention and extension. In addition, they reflect on their instructional strategies and make commitments to improving their practice.	☑ 1 ☐ 2 ☐ 3 ☐ 4 ☐ 5	This team is ranked as the most effective because the team focuses on the four critical questions of a PLC. The focus is on the learning of every student, sharing that responsibility, and changing adult practice.
Team C This team comes to each meeting already knowing what the focus will be. When this team decides to use a common assessment, they bring necessary data to the next meeting. Based on that assessment data, they discuss strategies they can use in their classrooms to address students in need of extra support.	☐ 1 ☑ 2 ☐ 3 ☐ 4 ☐ 5	This team is ranked second as there is a focus on using data from assessments to intervene. However, there is no mention of extension, sharing responsibility, or changes in adult practice.
Team D This team meets weekly. The focus of each meeting is determining essential standards, unpacking those standards, and developing common proficiency. This team uses this information to guide their work in individual classrooms.	☐ 1 ☐ 2 ☑ 3 ☐ 4 ☐ 5	This team is ranked third as the focus is on one question, question 1 of a PLC. The team has not yet moved to using their responses to this question for collaborative assessments or other work of effective teams.
Team E This team only comes to a meeting when they know their supervising administrator will be attending. At those meetings, which occur about once per month, they focus on pacing for an upcoming unit of study.	☐ 1 ☐ 2 ☐ 3 ☐ 4 ☑ 5	This team is ranked as least effective as the team only meets out of obligation, and their meeting time is irregular. In addition, the focus of these irregular meetings is not on the critical work of effective teams.

Propel Your PLC at Work © 2025 Solution Tree Press • SolutionTree.com
Visit **go.SolutionTree.com/PLCbooks** to download this free reproducible.

Doing the Work: Critical Considerations of a Collaborative Team

Critical Consideration	How I Suggest My Team Address This Consideration	Additions or Corrections Based on Discussion
Establish norms or working agreements to ensure the entire team has clarity for the behaviors expected.		
Be clear about the focus of each meeting.		
Practice and embrace the sharing of data.		
Discuss and learn to embrace dissonance.		
Embrace professionalism.		

Propel Your PLC at Work © 2025 Solution Tree Press • SolutionTree.com
Visit **go.SolutionTree.com/PLCbooks** to download this free reproducible.

Doing the Work: Critical Considerations of a Collaborative Team Key

Critical Consideration	How I Suggest My Team Address This Consideration
Establish norms or working agreements to ensure the entire team has clarity for the behaviors expected.	My team, at the beginning of the year, establishes norms through a collaborative process. We use a process, such as the one outlined in *Learning by Doing* (DuFour et al., 2024), to complete this task and revisit them regularly.
Be clear about the focus of each meeting.	My team ensures there is an agenda template ready to go and used for each meeting. The agenda is aligned to the four critical questions of a PLC rather than business items. This agenda is created in advance of the meeting and is distributed to the entire team.
Practice and embrace the sharing of data.	My team will establish a process for analyzing common assessment data that allows us to identify and provide the support students need. In addition, the process will ensure team members share what they did that was successful and what they would do differently to support students.
Discuss and learn to embrace dissonance.	My team makes plans to discuss how we will be able to have productive conversations even when we disagree. When we have disagreements, we name those disagreements and ensure our conversations stay on our ideas or thoughts and not on people.
Embrace professionalism.	My team will regularly reflect on what we have done to grow as educators by sharing what we have learned and how we have changed our practice, resulting in greater outcomes for students.

Chapter Four

Critical Question One

This chapter supports learning about how collaborative teams focus on learning in a PLC at Work. This is done by responding to critical question one of a PLC, which asks what educators want students to know and be able to do. Understanding this question is vital because collaborative teams use it to become clear about common learning expectations, and it provides the foundation for the remaining three critical questions of a PLC at Work. For example, without a common definition of proficiency, how can the teams build a common assessment? Or, without knowing the timing of which students should have mastered an essential skill, how will a team know when to intervene?

Determining essential standards, breaking those essentials into learning targets, and developing a definition of proficiency clarifies what each teacher and each student are expected to do. In addition, using these standards and learning targets to inform the scope and sequence of courses is important as it builds a guaranteed and viable curriculum. Educators performing these tasks as a team also builds ownership. Effective teams take time to answer thoroughly, check their results, and show flexibility in instruction.

Understanding Critical Question One

Critical question one asks, "What knowledge, skills, and dispositions should every student acquire as a result of this unit, this course, or this grade level" (DuFour et al., 2024, p. 44)? All collaborative teams in a school must answer this question about academic content. Yes, third-grade teachers must process this question for their mathematics curriculum, and high school social studies teachers must answer this question for civics. However, a schoolwide behavior team must also answer this question for schoolwide expected behaviors, and site intervention teams must answer this question to prioritize their finite intervention resources. This complex question is a logical starting point for teams to develop a common curriculum and learning goals. That common curriculum is guaranteed and viable:

> *Guaranteed* means that all teachers who teach the same levels or courses teach the same content. The content students learn does not vary depending on the teachers they are assigned. *Viable* means that the content is teachable in the time available. (Simms, 2024, p. 71)

Collaboration allows teachers to share their thinking, gain the perspectives of their peers, and use that knowledge in support of each other. Time dedicated to collaboration, however, must be spent on meaningful actions that lead to higher levels of learning (Simms, 2024). Teams developing a guaranteed and viable curriculum that they collectively implement is one of those meaningful actions. If teams do not plan and implement a common curriculum, assessments, and proficiency levels, and implement other knowledge gained as a team, they will be unable to collaboratively analyze their practice. They will not have a common base for the analysis. Without this analysis, adult practices will not change and, thus, student results will go unchanged.

Critical question one can be rephrased as *What do we need to determine for our learning expectations to be explicitly clear for each grade level, course, and unit of study?* To accomplish this task, teams must determine essential standards and associated learning targets, define proficiency, and develop appropriate scope and sequence. It certainly can be daunting work. However, the best method is just to begin. After teams have their first iteration complete, they will be more comfortable with the process and engage in regular—at least annual—refinements over time. This section provides a general understanding of question one.

Note that this text is written in the context of a collaborative team formed around teachers who share a common course or content. However, this is only a percentage of teams. Vertical or cross-discipline teams apply the same principles to the learning they are emphasizing as a team.

Essential Standards

Educators are tasked with educating students on a tremendous number of content and skills. This extends beyond just the subject area of a course. Educators are also responsible for teaching social-emotional (behavioral) skills and teaching academic (executive) skills. Yes, teachers are responsible for fostering learning across many areas. No, it doesn't have to be unbearable. Steps can make focused teaching more feasible. Without such steps, educators cannot ensure learning—only content coverage.

Prioritization, the first step in becoming explicitly clear about learning as a team, occurs when determining essential standards. This is true for content standards as well as behavioral standards. Determining which standards are essential for student success informs educators which standards they should emphasize, closely assess, and intervene on when students don't achieve proficiency. Education author Larry Ainsworth (2015) provides the following criteria to determine which standards are a priority.

- **Endurance:** Necessary beyond the unit or the course (The standard is reasonably needed for college or career success because the skill is foundational—for example, comparing and contrasting is a common social studies and English language arts standard that is necessary for college and career success.)
- **Leverage:** Applicable across subject areas (The standard is reasonably useful for success across content areas—for example,

comparing and contrasting are necessary for social studies and English language arts success, but it also meaningfully applies to science, foreign language, career and technical education courses, and more.)

- **Readiness:** Is a prerequisite skill for future essential learning (The standard is not only useful in the future or across disciplines, but it is also critical for success in the coursework of the discipline—for example, proficiently comparing and contrasting are necessary for analyzing multiple views of historical information in social studies courses at an increasingly complex level.)

Standards that have each of these characteristics—as determined by those *teaching* the skills—are deemed *essential*. (Generally, they must attain all three criteria to meet this.) Once they determine essentials, teams make certain teachers design instruction that ensures learning. This is one portion of a guaranteed and viable curriculum.

It is important those responsible for *teaching* the content have the dominant voice in determining what is deemed essential. These professionals are responsible for and take ownership of student learning, and this is why they are responsible for determining the focus. Additionally, prioritizing standards does not mean total omission of other (nonessential) standards. It is often a difference between what we are exposing students to and what we are ensuring mastery of. For example, a team may have an essential standard such as identifying the text's main point for English language arts. The team ensures this is taught and assessed and otherwise addressed with intention. The team may also have a standard that it incorporates but is less focused on monitoring and addressing (such as a standard on author's craft).

Learning Targets

Learning targets, associated with the identified essential standards, are the next task in building clarity on what we want students to know and be able to do. Learning targets build toward the standards, which are sometimes hard to decipher. Educator and author Nicole Dimich (2024) promotes unpacking standards and organizing them into so-called *progression ladders* in order of complexity. The process of breaking down standards as a team leads to clarity for the team. An additional consideration for developing learning targets includes using student-friendly language. This not only allows students to access learning goals, but it also allows them to self-assess these smaller components of learning to track progress.

Proficiency

The movement toward clarity begins with teams determining essential standards. It is then enhanced by breaking down those standards into clear learning targets. The clarifying work does not stop there.

The teams must establish a common definition for what success looks like. If a student meets the standard, what would that specifically look like? This is where teams determine what specific example mathematics problems learners need to practice or the criteria students need to produce. The teams will likely be using rubrics for assignments and assessments, and the proficient level language is created here. Determining proficiency ensures all educators teaching the same standards know what rigor to apply. Students will not be at the mercy of interpretation. Student A in class A and student B in class B are working toward the same specific goals.

Scope and Sequence

With essential standards, associated learning targets, and defined proficiency, the team has taken a significant leap toward responding to critical question one. They now must organize these pieces. This is where scope and sequence come in. If teams have a curricular resource, the collaborative teams analyze it to determine the following.

- **Where the standards and learning targets fit best:** They check for where the essentials currently are in the resource and determine if that corresponds to the appropriate intensity.
- **When they should ultimately be mastered:** They look where the resource provides instruction on the standards and determine at which point of this instruction students could reasonably be expected to be proficient. Many standards are not presented just one time but instead are presented multiple times at various depths. This is critical in later processes when it comes to intervening and extending.
- **What may have to be given up or deemphasized to ensure learning of the essentials:** They determine how much time students need to properly learn the essentials and plan more concise instruction for nonessential standards.

If there is not a primary course resource, teams can design units of study with the essentials in mind. This process ensures the curriculum is guaranteed and viable (Marzano, 2003).

Discussion Questions and Next Steps Resources

Consider these questions after reading this chapter

* Has your team worked on critical question one?
* Does your team have a process to revisit critical question one?
* Do all team members have the same understanding of how they are answering critical question one?

Suggested resources follow that can help you take next steps (if your existing PLC has not yet addressed those elements). These are in addition to the foundational texts mentioned in the introduction.

* Nicole Dimich's (2024) *Design in Five: Essential Phases to Create Engaging Assessment Practice,* Second Edition
* William M. Ferriter's (2020) *The Big Book of Tools for Collaborative Teams in a PLC at Work*
* Ferriter and colleagues' (2025) *The Big Book of Tools for RTI at Work*
* Maria Nielsen's (2024) *The 15-Day Challenge: Simplify and Energize Your PLC at Work Process*
* Anthony R. Reibel and colleagues' (2024) *Beyond PLC Lite*

Activities

Before moving on to the activities, ask participants to complete the reproducible "Topic Processing: Critical Question One" (page 68) to ensure they have a foundational understanding that allows them to apply their learning. Then have participants complete the reproducible "Analyzing the Current Reality: Critical Question One" (page 69). It will help you learn the team's implementation and response to that question and determine what may come next for them. To complete this tool, you may need to ask questions of your team and school leadership.

The following activities deepen a participant's understanding of critical question one. As the facilitator, you may choose to use one, some, or all of these learning opportunities based on need. In addition, you can modify any activity to meet adult learners' needs and facilitate engaged learning.

- **Scenarios: Critical Question One in a PLC at Work** helps participants differentiate between what teams do and do not focus on while establishing what they want students to know and be able to do. In this activity, participants read scenarios that share the actions of a collaborative team. They then use their knowledge to determine what from the provided scenario is and is not representative of critical question one. A possible extension for this activity is having participants rank the scenarios from most representative of a high-performing collaborative team to least representative.

- **Hit or Miss: Essential Standards** provides participants with an opportunity to develop their knowledge and skills around determining essential standards. In this activity, participants use the endurance, leverage, and readiness criteria to determine whether a provided standard is essential (hit) or not (miss). While a variety of standards are provided, the facilitator can easily exchange the provided standards for standards more relevant to participants. An answer key is not provided for this activity, as there is no right or wrong answer for what is essential. Collaborative teams must make these determinations through discussion and consensus.

- **Doing the Work: Critical Question One Example Process** deepens participants' understanding of the multiple elements involved in determining what they want students to know and be able to do. Participants practice the process by selecting an essential standard, unpacking the standard, and determining proficiency for the selected standard. While this is best completed as a collaborative activity among actual teams, this activity builds an understanding and confidence for doing the work. This activity can be particularly supportive for those who will or currently facilitate this process in collaborative teams.

> *Facilitating Professional Learning*
>
> **Consider the learning space.**
>
> Impactful professional learning requires participants to be able to focus, have discourse, and engage in the learning activities. Think about how the space should be designed for the best learning. This remains true for a virtual environment, as well. Make certain there is enough space for activities, set up the space for easy peer-to-peer or small-group discussion, and limit distractions. This does not mean the space needs to be a brick walled conference room with no windows. It does mean the facilitator should arrange the learning space to reduce the barriers that may be present for participants engaging in the learning activity.

Scenarios: Critical Question One in a PLC at Work

In this activity, participants review scenarios and identify what parts represent critical question one in a PLC at Work and what parts do not. While some of the scenarios may seem obvious, it is the discussion of *why* that makes this learning activity meaningful.

Follow these steps.

1. Before beginning, ensure some type of professional learning was shared to support the participants' understanding. This may be reading and debriefing this chapter's text.

2. Provide each participant with a copy of "Scenarios: Critical Question One in a

PLC at Work" (page 70) or display for all to read. Keep a copy of "Scenarios: Critical Question One in a PLC at Work Key" (page 72) for yourself to support discussion.

3. Ensure each participant has a partner or group to engage with. Cap groups at four people to allow effective discussion.

4. One round at a time, have participants read a scenario. Participants then, in the What Is Representative of a PLC and What Is *Not* Representative of a PLC columns, record details from the scenarios accordingly. Ask participants to refrain from moving on to the next round when they are done.

5. After each participant has read the scenario and recorded their rationale, they discuss with their partner or group. This can include the facilitator checking for consensus on the rationale and engaging in conversation where there may be disagreement. For example, you may ask for participants to share their answer, the rationale for their answer, and doubts about their answer.

6. If there is more than one group of participants, facilitate a whole-group conversation to see if there is consensus or dissonance on the rationale.

7. Provide the group with the answers from "Scenarios: Critical Question One in a PLC at Work Key" to spur further conversation.

8. Pending the group's answers, further discussion may be needed to provide a deeper understanding of the suggested answers and evidence. For example, if there are significant disagreements or misunderstandings, the facilitator may need to refer to resources on the concept to provide participants additional opportunities to learn.

9. Proceed to subsequent rounds, repeating the process.

Hit or Miss: Essential Standards

In this activity, participants review example standards and determine if they are essential. Using the idea of the game *Battleship*, standards considered essential are a hit, and those considered to not be essential are a miss. This activity has no answer key because responses vary depending on the district, school, and team. In addition, the facilitator can exchange the provided examples for local standards that fit and more deeply engage participants.

Follow these steps.

1. Before beginning, ensure some type of professional learning was shared to support the participants' understanding. This may be reading and debriefing this chapter's text.

2. Provide each participant with a copy of "Hit or Miss: Essential Standards" (page 74) or display for all to read.

3. Ensure that each participant has a partner or group to engage with. Cap groups at four people to allow effective discussion.

4. One round at a time, have participants read a standard. In the What Criteria This Standard Meets column, they check mark whether each has endurance, leverage, and readiness. Based on this analysis, participants determine if the standard is a hit (essential standard) or a miss (not an essential standard). Reiterate that, generally, standards must meet all three criteria to be essential.

5. After each participant has finished, they discuss with their partner or group.

6. If there is more than one group of participants, facilitate a whole-group conversation to see if there is consensus or dissonance on the rationale.

7. Pending the group's answers, further discussion may be needed to provide a deeper understanding of the suggested

answers and evidence. For example, if there are significant disagreements or misunderstandings, the facilitator may need to refer to resources on the concept to provide participants additional opportunities to learn.

8. Proceed to subsequent rounds, repeating the process.

Doing the Work: Critical Question One Example Process

In this activity, participants review example standards and choose one they believe is essential. They then unpack that standard into learning targets and determine an example of proficiency. There are no suggested answers, as answers will vary for the context of the district, school, or team. In addition, the provided examples can be swapped out for local standards that fit the participants.

Follow these steps.

1. Before beginning, ensure some type of professional learning was shared to support the participants' understanding. This may be reading and debriefing this chapter's text.

2. Provide each participant with a copy of "Doing the Work: Critical Question One Example Process" (page 75) or display for all to read.

3. Ensure each participant has a partner or group to engage with. Cap groups at four people to allow effective discussion.

4. For step 1 in the handout, participants use Ainsworth's (2015) three criteria of (1) endurance, (2) leverage, and (3) readiness to choose and circle a standard. Note that they may deem more than one standard essential. They should work with only one here.

5. For step 2 on the handout, each participant unpacks their chosen standard into the different skills or actions—learning targets—a student needs to obtain proficiency.

6. For step 3 on the handout, each participant writes what a student would show the teacher to demonstrate proficiency in the standard. Participants may write a description or use bullet points.

7. Individual participants, after completing this exercise, discuss their answers and rationale. Encourage a collaborative discussion.

Note the following effective modifications for this activity.

- Instead of completing this activity as an individual and then discussing, a partnership, small group, or a large group could make selections and discuss step by step.

- Instead of using the provided sample standards, standards could be swapped out for standards meaningful to the participants.

Topic Processing: Critical Question One

Is this a success area or a growth area for me, my team, or my school, and why?	What are my next steps to grow in my understanding?	Where can I get support to grow?

Propel Your PLC at Work © 2025 Solution Tree Press • SolutionTree.com
Visit **go.SolutionTree.com/PLCbooks** to download this free reproducible.

Analyzing the Current Reality: Critical Question One

To complete this tool, you may need to ask questions of your team and school leadership. Doing so will assist your understanding and help you learn what may come next for your team. The evidence column allows you to provide specific evidence of the current reality.

Critical Consideration	Current Reality	Evidence
My team has analyzed standards and determined which are most critical for student learning (essential standards).	☐ Not at all true. ☐ Somewhat true. ☐ Mostly true. ☐ Always true.	
My team has unpacked essential standards into student-friendly learning targets.	☐ Not at all true. ☐ Somewhat true. ☐ Mostly true. ☐ Always true.	
My team has determined what proficiency looks like for each essential standard, providing clarity around what students should know and be able to do.	☐ Not at all true. ☐ Somewhat true. ☐ Mostly true. ☐ Always true.	
My team has determined when teachers are expected to instruct and students are expected to master essential standards.	☐ Not at all true. ☐ Somewhat true. ☐ Mostly true. ☐ Always true.	
My team has calibrated how we will determine proficiency on essentials.	☐ Not at all true. ☐ Somewhat true. ☐ Mostly true. ☐ Always true.	

Propel Your PLC at Work © 2025 Solution Tree Press • SolutionTree.com
Visit **go.SolutionTree.com/PLCbooks** to download this free reproducible.

Scenarios: Critical Question One in a PLC at Work

Scenario	What Is Representative of a PLC	What Is Not Representative of a PLC
Round one A team is working on determining essential standards for their common course of study. To do so, they look at other schools who have done this work and professional organizations for their content area. As a result, they vote to adopt one of the prioritized standards sets they found.		
Round two A team has identified essential standards. In addition, they have developed learning targets associated with each. They have used this information to develop common assessments. There is evidence that students doing the same level of work are getting different feedback or scores.		
Round three A team has determined essential standards for a course they have in common. Each teacher decides how and when they will teach the essentials. The team will evaluate success at the end of the school year.		

Propel Your PLC at Work © 2025 Solution Tree Press • SolutionTree.com
Visit **go.SolutionTree.com/PLCbooks** to download this free reproducible.

Round four A team understands they must prioritize standards as they are not able to teach all standards to mastery. To prioritize, they look at their textbook series to see which standards have the most time dedicated to them.		
Round five A team of content teachers has taken their essential standards and unpacked them into learning targets. For each standard, they have developed rubric language to establish what proficiency in the standard means.		

Scenarios: Critical Question One in a PLC at Work Key

Scenario	What Is Representative of a PLC	What Is Not Representative of a PLC
Round one A team is working on determining essential standards for their common course of study. To do so, they look at other schools who have done this work and professional organizations for their content area. As a result, they vote to adopt one of the prioritized standards sets they found.	This team demonstrates understanding that essential standards are important, and they do a great deal of research on standards.	This team relies on external tools and organizations to determine their standards rather than using effective collaborative processes and professional judgment that build educator commitment.
Round two A team has identified essential standards. In addition, they have developed learning targets associated with each. They have used this information to develop common assessments. There is evidence that students doing the same level of work are getting different feedback or scores.	This team has demonstrated the importance of determining essential standards, unpacking those standards, and using common assessments.	This team does not appear to have established a common definition of proficiency, hampering their effectiveness.
Round three A team has determined essential standards for a course they have in common. Each teacher decides how and when they will teach the essentials. The team will evaluate success at the end of the school year.	This team has demonstrated they know the importance of essential standards and that success must be measured.	This team has not established a common understanding of when essentials will be taught, leaving success up to chance.

Propel Your PLC at Work © 2025 Solution Tree Press • SolutionTree.com
Visit **go.SolutionTree.com/PLCbooks** to download this free reproducible.

Round four A team understands they must prioritize standards as they are not able to teach all standards to mastery. To prioritize, they look at their textbook series to see which standards have the most time dedicated to them.	This team understands they need to determine essentials in order to ensure learning over just coverage of content.	This team's protocol does not include a useful protocol to determine essentials. Instead, they rely on a purchased resource and not a collaborative process, which is more meaningful to those involved.
Round five A team of content teachers has taken their essential standards and unpacked them into learning targets. For each standard, they have developed rubric language to establish what proficiency in the standard means.	A collaborative team is established, determines essentials, and develops a common language for proficiency.	This team is made up of content teachers and could include other key staff, including special education teachers or English language learning teachers, to enhance their work. In addition, they could calibrate their proficiency on the rubric language by using student work samples.

Hit or Miss: Essential Standards

Standard	What Criteria This Standard Meets (Ainsworth, 2015)	This Is an Essential Standard
Round one **Content Area:** Social Studies **Grade Level:** 8 **Standard:** Make a claim based on a debatable question with evidence provided from two or more sources.	☐ Endurance ☐ Leverage ☐ Readiness	☐ **Hit:** This is an essential standard. ☐ **Miss:** This is not an essential standard.
Round two **Content Area:** Science **Grade Level:** 3 **Standard:** Use patterns in graphs, charts, or results of experiments to make predictions.	☐ Endurance ☐ Leverage ☐ Readiness	☐ **Hit:** This is an essential standard. ☐ **Miss:** This is not an essential standard.
Round three **Content Area:** Mathematics **Grade Level:** 1 **Standard:** Tell time using both digital and analog clocks when provided on the hour or on the half hour examples.	☐ Endurance ☐ Leverage ☐ Readiness	☐ **Hit:** This is an essential standard. ☐ **Miss:** This is not an essential standard.
Round four **Content Area:** Literacy **Grade Level:** 10 **Standard:** Explain how a character in a piece of literature develops over time, providing specific evidence of character development.	☐ Endurance ☐ Leverage ☐ Readiness	☐ **Hit:** This is an essential standard. ☐ **Miss:** This is not an essential standard.
Round five **Content Area:** Career and technical education; music; art **Grade Level:** 6 **Standard:** After creating, performing, or demonstrating, clearly explain the process used to complete the task both verbally and in writing.	☐ Endurance ☐ Leverage ☐ Readiness	☐ **Hit:** This is an essential standard. ☐ **Miss:** This is not an essential standard.

Ainsworth, L. (2015). Priority standards: The power of focus. Accessed at www.edweek.org/education/opinion-priority-standards-the-power-of-focus/2015/02 on May 8, 2024.

Doing the Work: Critical Question One Example Process

Step 1: Choose one of the listed standards from the four listed below that you consider to be an essential standard. Use the criteria of endurance, leverage, and readiness to make your determination. Make your selection by circling the standard.

Standard A	**Standard B**	**Standard C**	**Standard D**
Students will be able to state a claim and provide an explanation verbally when asked a question about a topic with which they are familiar.	Students will be able to locate relevant resources, analyze those resources, and use those resources to state a written claim, citing specific evidence when provided a topic with multiple viewpoints.	Students will be able to provide written feedback to peers on verbal or written products when provided success criteria.	Students will be able to track their own progress toward personal goals that they have established, adjusting their action plans as needed.

Step 2: For your chosen standard, unpack the standard into learning targets. To assist with this, you can think of all the steps a student would need to know or do to reach this standard.

Step 3: For your chosen standard, based on the clarity developed in the learning target process, record your definition of proficiency. In other words, what would student work look or sound like to show they have met the standard? This could be a sample problem, proficient rubric language, or another tactic that will lead to a clear definition of proficiency.

Propel Your PLC at Work © 2025 Solution Tree Press • SolutionTree.com
Visit **go.SolutionTree.com/PLCbooks** to download this free reproducible.

Chapter Five

Critical Question Two

Clearly establishing what we want students to know and be able to do provides teachers and students with clarity. This can immediately improve student outcomes. However, stopping there sells the system and our potential impact short. We must also collaboratively design high-quality assessments that lead to specific, timely feedback to students and a look at results. Critical question two embodies the big idea of focusing on results.

This chapter supports learning how collaborative teams focus on determining whether students have met learning goals in a PLC at Work. This is done by answering critical question two of a PLC. Collaborative teams use this question to establish assessments, formal or informal, to determine whether students have met the desired level of rigor. Critical question two builds on critical question one (page 61) and sets the stage for the remaining two.

Understanding Critical Question Two

Clear learning goals are helpful in narrowing down our instruction and ensuring we have a guaranteed and viable curriculum. An effective team, however, doesn't stop there. The team answers the question, "How will we know when each student has acquired the essential knowledge and skills" (DuFour et al., 2024, p. 44)? In other words, what methods will the team use to see if students are meeting essential learning goals? This is the assessment question. Various forms of assessment can be used, but we must gather evidence to check on learning. Traditional paper and pencil assessments, performance assessments, observations, and exit tickets, to name a few, are all acceptable. Not using evidence can cause a whole host of issues, including unintentionally inserting bias in the process.

Note that this section is written with the assumption that a collaborative team is formed around teachers who share a common course or content. However, vertical or cross-discipline teams apply the same principles to what they are emphasizing as a team in cycles of learning.

Assessment Design

Assessment design is something educators are perfectly capable of despite it potentially feeling complex. As they design, they remember that collected information must do two things: (1) inform the educator of next steps for instruction and (2) provide feedback to students. Traditional assessments, by only providing a percentage of "correct" answers or a similarly simple score, do neither of these.

Several well-researched models embody meaningful assessment design, and some suggestions follow.

1. Design the end-of-unit assessment before starting to teach the unit of study (Wiggins & McTighe, 2005). This *backward design* ensures each educator teaching the course is clear on the outcomes and rigor expected for all students.

2. Design the assessment to report by learning target (Grant, Hindman, & Stronge, 2010). This means that students, as a result of the assessment, get information in relation to their proficiency on *each assessed learning target* rather than as an overall percentage or number of correct answers. In addition, teachers get the data they need to plan the most effective and targeted next step.

3. Use the end-of-unit assessment to inform formative learning checks along the way (Bailey & Jakicic, 2023). Designing and delivering these smaller assessments aligned to the end-of-unit assessment gives educators and students timely feedback. That means students can correct before end-of-unit assessments.

4. Ensure that the types of tasks assigned on an assessment appropriately match the learning target it is expected to assess (Dimich, 2024). For example, using a matching activity when the standard or target demands analysis is unlikely to accurately determine proficiency on the intended skill.

Multiple choice, short answer, written response, and performance tasks are all valid in assessment design, provided that the learning target can be effectively measured through that method. Using these concepts as you reflect on assessment design can be a leap forward.

Feedback

The assessment process, whether formative or summative, must include feedback for learners. Research makes it clear that feedback on student work has a profound impact on learning (Hattie, 2023). Feedback can occur through many methods (some mentioned in the previous section) and be embedded in daily instruction. Feedback to assessment embedded in daily instruction can include individual or whole-class responses to teacher questions, teachers providing supportive prompts to students based on observations made during class, and clarifying instruction based on student performance.

However, assessments that do not provide powerful feedback to students are ineffective and devour time. It takes time to assess, but when the feedback accompanying the assessment results amounts to "Good work," "Try again," or "This is unclear," students have nowhere to go to revisit or extend their learning (as covered in chapters 6 and 7, pages 95 and 113).

Such statements are not feedback but simply praise or criticism.

Educators and authors Garnet Hillman and Mandy Stalets (2019) share that effective feedback comes in the following forms.

- **Sharing strengths:** For example, "Your paragraph in response to the prompt is concise and provides specific details to support your claim."
- **Connecting that strength to the learning targets:** For example, "The learning target calls for being concise and for using specific details, which you demonstrated the ability to do. The learning target also calls for writing with clarity."
- **Providing the next step for growth:** For example, "To improve your paragraph in this example and in the future, it would be beneficial to reread the paragraph and ask yourself if your peers would understand what you are trying to say. While you may know what you are trying to articulate, pretend as though the concept you are sharing is new to you. Would that change your writing?"

This feedback can be provided through written notes, rubrics, conferences, and other methods. If providing feedback is overwhelming, educators may need to look at the frequency of assessments and how many learning targets are being assessed. Focus can provide the opportunity for students and teachers to perform at higher, and more attainable, levels.

Data Analysis

Teacher analysis and the resulting actions plans, preferably involving collaboration with collaborative team members, is where assessment can go from supporting learning to accelerating learning. Ensuring that assessments are designed to collect evidence of proficiency on each assessed learning target is a crucial prerequisite to analysis. If this is done, data analysis can be an efficient process.

Data analysis involves some key questions that support teacher and student next steps. That analysis comes at two levels.

1. **The first analysis level is on the assessments overall:** Were there targets on which many students were not successful in attaining proficiency? Were there targets on which most students were successful? These questions, including analyzing the why behind the answers, will inform next steps in universal instruction.

2. **The second analysis level is a student-by-student plan:** For each learning target deemed essential enough to assess, how will educators respond to those students who have not met proficiency? For those students who have demonstrated success, how will we ensure they continue to grow? The result should be a listing of students by target who need intervention and those who could benefit from a learning extension.

This list is necessary when answering critical questions three (chapter 6, page 95) and four (chapter 7, page 113) of the PLC process.

> ## Discussion Questions and Next Steps Resources
>
> **Consider these questions after reading this chapter.**
>
> * Do your assessment practices provide feedback to students and to the teacher?
> * Does your team analyze assessments together?
> * What are the next steps to strengthen assessment practices with your team?
>
> Suggested resources follow that can help you take next steps (if your existing PLC has not yet addressed those elements). These are in addition to the foundational texts mentioned in the introduction.
>
> * Kim Bailey and Chris Jakicic's (2023) *Common Formative Assessment, Second* Edition
> * Damian Cooper's (2022) *Rebooting Assessment: A Practical Guide for Balancing Conversations, Performances, and Products*
> * Eileen Depka's (2019) *Letting Data Lead: How to Design, Analyze, and Respond to Classroom Assessment*
> * Nicole Dimich's (2024) *Design in Five: Essential Phases to Create Engaging Assessment Practice*, Second Edition
> * Nicole Dimich and colleagues' (2022) *Concise Answers to Frequently Asked Questions About Assessment and Grading*
> * Garnet Hillman and Mandy Stalets's (2019) *Coaching Your Classroom: How to Deliver Actionable Feedback to Students*

Activities

Before moving on to the activities, ask participants to complete the reproducible "Topic Processing: Critical Question Two" (page 84) to ensure they have a foundational understanding that allows them to apply their learning. Then have participants complete the reproducible "Analyzing the Current Reality: Critical Question Two" (page 85). It will help you learn the team's implementation of and response to that question and determine what may come next for them. To complete this tool, you may need to ask questions of your team and school leadership.

The following activities deepen a participant's understanding of critical question two. As the facilitator, you may choose to use one, some, or all of these learning opportunities based on need. In addition, you can modify any activity to meet adult learners' needs and facilitate engaged learning.

- **Scenarios: Critical Question Two in a PLC at Work** helps develop a deeper understanding of how teams collaborate to establish how they will determine if students have learned essential skills. To do so, this activity uses scenarios. Participants read each scenario and determine what is representative and what is not representative of a team's work with critical question two in a PLC at Work. While participants can record their answers in the provided graphic organizer, this activity can be enhanced with opportunities for discussion.

- **Thumbs-Up or Thumbs-Down: Critical Question Two in a PLC at Work** deepens participant understanding by asking them to analyze possible team actions related to establishing assessments and determining how to use assessments. This activity involves participants giving a thumbs-up to a concept if, based on their established knowledge, it is an effective or appropriate action. On the contrary, participants can give the concept a thumbs-down if they determine it to be ineffective or inappropriate action. A graphic organizer is provided so participants can capture a rationale for their answer. The facilitator orchestrates opportunities for collaboration and discussion embedded in the activity.

- **Doing the Work: Data Analysis** provides an opportunity for participants to practice analyzing a set of assessment data. In addition, they will use that data to plan for student support. This activity knowingly blends the work of critical questions one, two, and three of a PLC at Work. The facilitator can provide further context by identifying an essential standard or learning target relevant to participants. If a team is new to the process, the provided reproducible can help guide a team through its own actual data.

> ### Facilitating Professional Learning
>
> **Open time for dialogue.**
>
> Professional learning that leads to any impactful change requires the opportunity for participants to process the information they're learning. Providing opportunities for participants to parse aloud what they have learned, particularly about how they can apply the learning, can be effective (Zwiers & Crawford, 2023). However, facilitators must be wary of overplanning professional learning and packing in too much information. Doing that cuts necessary opportunities to process learning and unintentionally reduces the participants' chance to learn the information.

Scenarios: Critical Question Two in a PLC at Work

In this activity, participants review scenarios to discuss and identify what parts of the scenario represent an understanding of critical question two in a PLC at Work and what parts do not. While some of the scenarios may seem obvious, it is the discussion of *why* that makes this learning activity meaningful.

Follow these steps.

1. Before beginning, ensure some type of professional learning was shared to support the participants' understanding. This may be reading and debriefing this chapter's text.
2. Provide each participant with a copy of "Scenarios: Critical Question Two in a PLC at Work" (page 86) or display for all to read. Keep a copy of "Scenarios: Critical Question Two in a PLC at Work Key" (page 88) for yourself to support discussion.
3. Ensure each participant has a partner or group to engage with. Cap groups at four people to allow effective discussion.
4. One round at a time, have participants read a scenario. Participants then, in the What Is Representative of a PLC and What Is *Not* Representative of a PLC columns, record details from the scenarios accordingly. Ask participants to refrain from moving on to the next round when they are done.
5. After each participant has read the scenario and recorded their rationale, they discuss it with their partner or group. This can include the facilitator checking for consensus on the rationale and engaging in conversation where there may be disagreement. For example, you may ask for participants to share their answer, the rationale for their answer, and doubts about their answer.
6. If there is more than one group of participants, facilitate a whole-group conversation to see if there is consensus or dissonance on the rationale.
7. Provide the group with the answers from "Scenarios: Critical Question Two in a PLC at Work Key" to spur further conversation.
8. Pending the group's answers, further discussion may be needed to provide a deeper understanding of the suggested answers and evidence. For example, if there are significant disagreements or misunderstandings, the facilitator may need to refer to resources on the concept to provide participants additional opportunities to learn.
9. Proceed to subsequent rounds, repeating the process.

Thumbs-Up or Thumbs-Down: Critical Question Two in a PLC at Work

In this activity, participants look at possible elements that align to critical question two in a PLC at Work. They will determine if this is a good practice (thumbs-up) or a poor practice (thumbs-down). While some of the elements may seem obvious, it is the discussion of *why* that makes this learning activity meaningful.

Follow these steps.

1. Before beginning, ensure some type of professional learning was shared to support the participants' understanding. This may be reading and debriefing this chapter's text.

2. Provide each participant with a copy of "Thumbs-Up or Thumbs-Down: Critical Question Two in a PLC at Work" (page 90) or display for all to read. Keep a copy of "Thumbs-Up or Thumbs-Down: Critical Question Two in a PLC at Work Key" (page 91) for yourself to support discussion.

3. Ensure each participant has a partner or group to engage with. Cap groups at four people to allow effective discussion.

4. One round at a time, readers read each concept. In the Thumbs-Up or Thumbs-Down column, they check mark if the concept aligns with critical question two in a PLC at Work (thumbs-up) or does not align (thumbs-down). They also write their rationale for the decision in that column.

5. After each participant has read the scenario and recorded their rationale, they discuss with their partner or group. This can include checking for consensus on their rationale and discussing disagreements.

6. If there is more than one group of participants, facilitate a whole-group conversation to see if there is consensus or dissonance on the rationale.

7. Provide the group with the answers from "Thumbs-Up or Thumbs-Down: Critical Question Two in a PLC at Work Key" to spur further conversation.

8. Pending the group's answers, further discussion may be needed to provide a deeper understanding of the suggested answers and evidence. For example, if there are significant disagreements or misunderstandings, the facilitator may need to refer to resources on the concept to provide participants additional opportunities to learn.

9. Proceed to subsequent rounds, repeating the process.

Doing the Work: Data Analysis

In this activity, participants analyze an assessment. They pretend the assessment data for a group of three teachers have already been recorded, and participants focus on how to use the data to move forward.

Follow these steps.

1. Before beginning, ensure some type of professional learning was shared to support the participants' understanding. This may be reading and debriefing this chapter's text.

2. Break participants into groups of three and provide each person a copy of "Doing the Work: Data Analysis" (page 92).

3. Participants each take on one of the roles (teacher A, B, or C), ensuring each role is represented by a group member. These teacher roles are indicated in step 1 on "Doing the Work: Data Analysis."

4. Participants review the information for step 1 to orient themselves to the data.

5. Since there are two learning targets on the assessment in this scenario, the group discusses actions they could take to address students' needs who *have not yet* demonstrated proficiency for each learning target. They record these ideas in step 2.

6. The group writes how they can address the needs of students who *have* demonstrated proficiency for each learning target. They record these ideas in step 3.

7. The groups create an action plan in step 4. They determine who will complete what action on what timeline for each learning target, for students who are *not yet* proficient, and for students who *are* proficient.

8. The facilitator can support a whole-group conversation about the developed ideas for each target for intervention and extension to enhance all toolboxes.

Note that because this is a simulation, teams can take liberties to fill in the gaps. The emphasis should be twofold: that the team, in collaboration, (1) shares ideas on how to support all students and (2) commits to taking action. In addition, the facilitator may exchange the listed targets with targets that may be more meaningful for their setting, such as those adopted in the school or those that form the participating team's content area, to make this activity more relevant to the participants.

Topic Processing: Critical Question Two

Is this a success area or a growth area for me, my team, or my school, and why?	What are my next steps to grow in my understanding?	Where can I get support to grow?

Propel Your PLC at Work © 2025 Solution Tree Press • SolutionTree.com
Visit **go.SolutionTree.com/PLCbooks** to download this free reproducible.

Analyzing the Current Reality: Critical Question Two

To complete this tool, you may need to ask questions of your team and school leadership. Doing so will assist your understanding and help you learn what may come next for your team. The evidence column allows you to provide specific evidence of the current reality.

Concept	Current Reality	Evidence
My team plans the end-of-unit assessment before the teaching of the unit begins.	☐ Not at all true. ☐ Somewhat true. ☐ Mostly true. ☐ Always true.	
My team designs assessments that report by learning targets and not with an overall score.	☐ Not at all true. ☐ Somewhat true. ☐ Mostly true. ☐ Always true.	
My team plans for formative checks for understanding throughout the unit.	☐ Not at all true. ☐ Somewhat true. ☐ Mostly true. ☐ Always true.	
My team designs assessments that provide feedback to both the teacher and the students.	☐ Not at all true. ☐ Somewhat true. ☐ Mostly true. ☐ Always true.	
My team analyzes assessment data together to determine improvements for adult practice and determine student needs.	☐ Not at all true. ☐ Somewhat true. ☐ Mostly true. ☐ Always true.	

Propel Your PLC at Work © 2025 Solution Tree Press • SolutionTree.com
Visit **go.SolutionTree.com/PLCbooks** to download this free reproducible.

Scenarios: Critical Question Two in a PLC at Work

Scenario	What Is Representative of a PLC at Work	What Is Not Representative of a PLC at Work
Round one A teacher writes an assessment before the unit of study begins. She uses the learning targets the team deemed to be critical for the unit of study and related to the essential standards. On the assessment, for each learning target assessed, a spot for the total number of items correct is provided.		
Round two A team develops an end-of-unit assessment that is based on two essential standards for the unit. In addition, they plan two formative assessments to deliver during the unit of study, informing them of student progress toward essentials. A common date is determined for the end-of-unit assessment.		
Round three As a team develops an assessment, they organize the assessment by essentials. At the end of each section, there is space for the teacher to provide feedback. The structure for providing feedback is focused on listing errors the student made in their work.		

Round four A team uses an assessment prepared by a textbook publisher. They agree on dates for the assessment and when they will analyze the data together. When they collaborate on results, they look at how many students got each question correct or incorrect.		
Round five A team is nearing the completion of a unit of study. They meet to write the end-of-unit assessment. They organize the assessment by essential standard, discuss what it means for a student to be proficient, and create a location on the assessment for feedback that indicates next steps a student can take for growth. The team agrees to deliver the assessment in two days.		

Scenarios: Critical Question Two in a PLC at Work Key

Scenario	What Is Representative of a PLC at Work	What Is Not Representative of a PLC at Work
Round one A teacher writes an assessment before the unit of study begins. She uses the learning targets the team deemed to be critical for the unit of study and related to the essential standards. On the assessment, for each learning target assessed, a spot for the total number of items correct is provided.	Essential standards were used to inform the assessment, and the scores are reported out by the learning target. In addition, the assessment is designed before the unit begins so instruction can be focused.	This assessment appears to be written and delivered by an individual rather than the team who determined essentials. In addition, there is no feedback provided to students outside of a total number correct.
Round two A team develops an end-of-unit assessment that is based on two essential standards for the unit. In addition, they plan two formative assessments to deliver during the unit of study, informing them of student progress toward essentials. A common date is determined for the end-of-unit assessment.	The team uses essentials to plan their end-of-unit assessment and formative assessments. In addition, a common date is planned for the end-of-unit assessment, allowing for the team to collaboratively analyze results.	It appears the team did not plan on common dates for formative assessments within the unit of study, which complicates collaboration on analyzing results.
Round three A team develops an assessment, they organize the assessment by essentials. At the end of each section, there is space for the teacher to provide feedback. The structure for providing feedback is focused on listing errors the student made in their work.	The team has organized their assessment by essential standard or target. In addition, there is intent to provide feedback.	The feedback provided to students focuses only on errors. There should be additional information making a connection to the essential learning and indicating the next step for growth.

Round four — A team uses an assessment prepared by a textbook publisher. They agree on dates for the assessment and when they will analyze the data together. When they collaborate on results, they look at how many students got each question correct or incorrect.	The team determined a common assessment and a date to deliver that assessment. In addition, they analyzed data together.	While using an assessment from a publisher is acceptable, the team did not organize or map the assessment to report out by essential learning. Therefore, the analysis is focused on each question rather than determining who was and was not proficient on a target or standard.
Round five — A team is nearing the completion of a unit of study. They meet to write the end-of-unit assessment. They organize the assessment by essential standard, discuss what it means for a student to be proficient, and create a location on the assessment for feedback that indicates next steps a student can take for growth. The team agrees to deliver the assessment in two days.	The team had a collaborative process to develop an assessment, determine proficiency, and provide feedback.	The team created the assessment at the end of the unit rather than prior to the unit, which means it was not available for assisting with instruction during the unit.

Thumbs-Up or Thumbs-Down: Critical Question Two in a PLC at Work

Concept	Thumbs-Up or Down	Rationale
Round one Design assessments to report out by total points or the percent correct.	☐ Thumbs-up ☐ Thumbs-down	
Round two Ensure there is an opportunity to provide feedback to students on each standard or target on an assessment.	☐ Thumbs-up ☐ Thumbs-down	
Round three Design the end-of-unit assessment before the unit begins.	☐ Thumbs-up ☐ Thumbs-down	
Round four Only end-of-unit assessments are needed to support instruction.	☐ Thumbs-up ☐ Thumbs-down	
Round five Use only written response questions for common assessments.	☐ Thumbs-up ☐ Thumbs-down	
Round six Feedback to students should be focused on errors made.	☐ Thumbs-up ☐ Thumbs-down	
Round seven In analyzing assessments, teams look both at how they can support students and how they can positively impact adult practices.	☐ Thumbs-up ☐ Thumbs-down	

Propel Your PLC at Work © 2025 Solution Tree Press • SolutionTree.com
Visit **go.SolutionTree.com/PLCbooks** to download this free reproducible.

Thumbs-Up or Thumbs-Down: Critical Question Two in a PLC at Work Key

Concept	Thumbs-Up or Down	Rationale
Round one Design assessments to report out by total points or the percent correct.	☐ Thumbs-up ☑ Thumbs-down	Assessments may report out by these indicators but should more importantly report out indicators if a student is proficient or not for each assessed standard or target.
Round two Ensure there is an opportunity to provide feedback to students on each standard or target on an assessment.	☑ Thumbs-up ☐ Thumbs-down	Feedback goes beyond providing a score and indicates what a student can do to improve.
Round three Design the end-of-unit assessment before the unit begins.	☑ Thumbs-up ☐ Thumbs-down	This provides the clarity for teachers to know what will be expected of students at the conclusion of the unit's learning.
Round four Only end-of-unit assessments are needed to support instruction.	☐ Thumbs-up ☑ Thumbs-down	End-of-unit assessments are important. However, using assessments to indicate progress within the unit of study will lead to a quicker adult reaction time and, therefore, higher levels of learning.
Round five Use only written response questions for common assessments.	☐ Thumbs-up ☑ Thumbs-down	While questions on assessments should best match the standards or targets, this does not always need to be a written response.
Round six Feedback to students should be focused on errors made.	☐ Thumbs-up ☑ Thumbs-down	Feedback should include strengths, connections to learning targets, and next steps. Just focusing on errors does not, necessarily, lead to growth.
Round seven In analyzing assessments, teams look both at how they can support students and how they can positively impact adult practices.	☑ Thumbs-up ☐ Thumbs-down	Teams should use assessments to decide who needs extension and intervention. However, there must also be conversation on how adult practice can change to better meet student needs.

Doing the Work: Data Analysis

Step 1: Based on the assessment delivered, two essential learning targets were assessed. Each of the three teachers on the team provided their data.

Learning Target	Teacher A	Teacher B	Teacher C
Target one Students can state a claim.	20 of 25 students were proficient.	22 of 25 students were proficient.	21 of 25 students were proficient.
Target two Students can provide a piece of evidence for a claim they have stated.	19 of 25 students were proficient.	16 of 25 students were proficient.	17 of 25 students were proficient.

Step 2: Each teacher, based on their data, had students who needed reteaching to meet the determined proficiency of the standard. They discuss how they can support students who need additional support to reach proficiency.

Target one Students can state a claim.	**Target two** Students can provide a piece of evidence for a claim they have stated.
The team determined the following strategies could be used to support students in need of extra time and support to reach proficiency:	The team determined the following strategies could be used to support students in need of extra time and support to reach proficiency:

Propel Your PLC at Work © 2025 Solution Tree Press • SolutionTree.com
Visit **go.SolutionTree.com/PLCbooks** to download this free reproducible.

Step 3: Each teacher, based on their data, had students who met proficiency of the standard. They discuss how they can deepen learning for students who have already demonstrated proficiency.

Target one Students can state a claim.	*Target two* Students can provide a piece of evidence for a claim they have stated.
The team determined the following strategies could be used to support students who already demonstrated proficiency:	The team determined the following strategies could be used to support students who already demonstrated proficiency:

Step 4: The team discusses how the team will ensure students receive what they need based on the assessment results. As the team has already discussed strategies, the team is now looking at who will do what by when to serve students.

Target one Students can state a claim.	*Target two* Students can provide a piece of evidence for a claim they have stated.
Who will do what by when to serve students not yet proficient in this target?	Who will do what by when to serve students not yet proficient in this target?
Who will do what by when to serve students already proficient in this target?	Who will do what by when to serve students already proficient in this target?

Chapter Six

Critical Question Three

Critical question three in a PLC at Work asks what teams will do if students have not learned the expected standards. Answering that question requires the big ideas of collaboration and a results focus; those two big ideas allow educators to embrace the first big idea, a focus on learning. Because response to intervention (RTI) encompasses all instructional levels in tiers 1, 2, and 3, individual teachers, collaborative teams, and schoolwide teams support this question.

The first focus in RTI is on high-quality Tier 1 instruction—the instruction that all students receive. Tier 2 instruction (targeted reteaching to small groups or individuals after proficiency is expected) and Tier 3 instruction (instruction or intensive instruction to address universal skill gaps) are critical to a system in addition to Tier 1 instruction. However, if schools find themselves focused on supporting individuals or student groups at the expense of universal instruction, it is time to reevaluate their Tier 1 practices. Teachers and collaborative teams who attempt to compensate for low-quality instruction by providing individual or small-group instruction will likely erode time dedicated to universal Tier 1 instruction and thus see further negative results.

This chapter deepens the understanding of how teams provide additional time and support for students to meet grade-level expectations. Determining support for students and adjustments is an important component of this question's answers. Content in this chapter builds off critical questions one and two.

Understanding Critical Question Three

Clear learning goals establish what schools want students to know and be able to do. Assessments ensure educators can determine which students meet which learning goals. Now, you arrive at critical question three of a PLC at Work: "How will we respond when some students do not learn" (DuFour et al., 2024, p. 44)? Educators often naturally observe, provide unit assessments, give quizzes, and maybe even pre-assess units. Responding to what they learn from assessments is the harder part. Action based on results is so integral to learning that educator and author Rick Wormeli (2018) emphasizes not taking the time to assess unless someone will take action based on the results.

Make no mistake: This question is about adult actions to ensure learning. It is not about making students responsible for why they did not learn. If we deem learning a specific skill enough of a priority to assess it, then we must deem it a priority to intervene when students do not demonstrate success. This intervention occurs across all three RTI tiers, which you can see in figure 6.1.

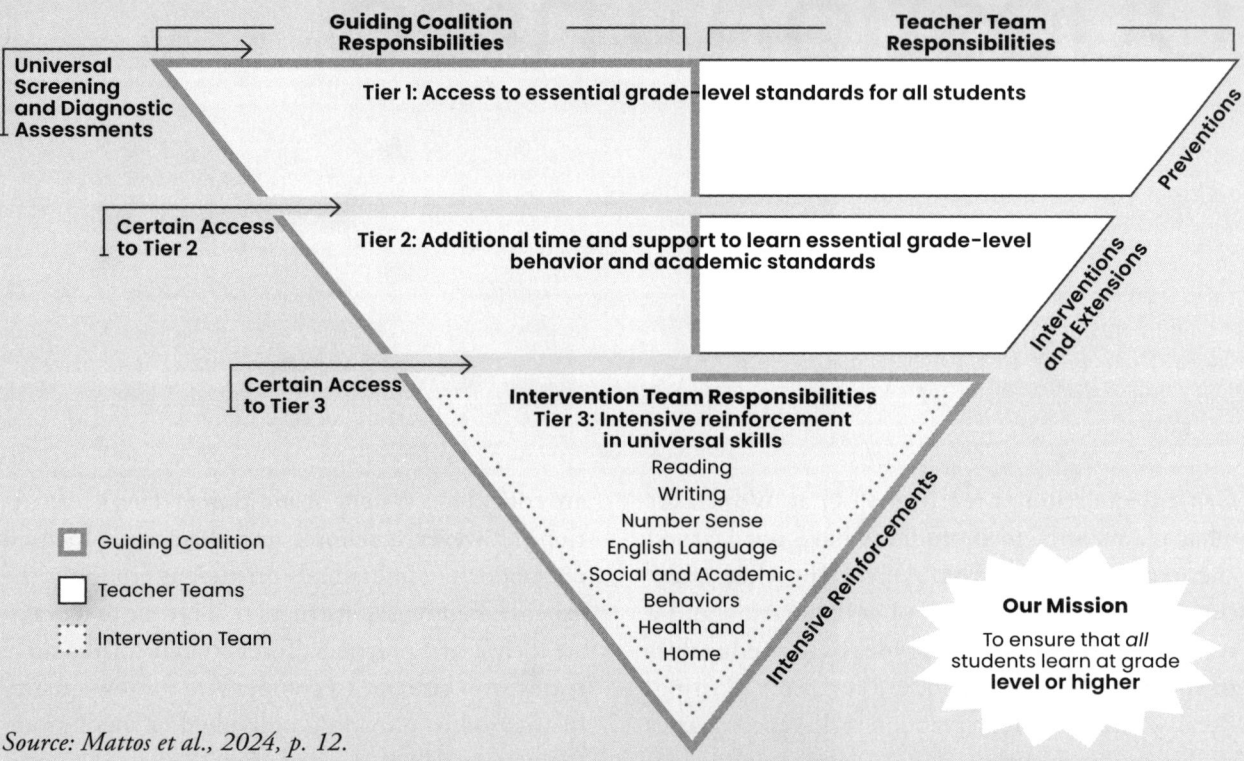

Source: Mattos et al., 2024, p. 12.

Figure 6.1: Response to intervention allows intensive reinforcement in universal skills.

In addition, it is important to understand that while time is dedicated to addressing student needs, it is not at the expense of essential grade-level learning. Tier 1 universal instruction, reducing the need for additional time and support, is critical.

Keep in mind that this text provides a general understanding of how teams respond to assessment data as a part of a process to support students learning at grade level or higher. Additionally, this text is written with the assumption that a collaborative team is formed around teachers who share a common course or content. However, vertical or cross-discipline teams apply the same principles to the learning they are emphasizing as a team.

Addressing Needs in Tier 1

In Tier 1—universal instruction every student receives—teachers can work to prevent the need for more intensive needs of support. To start, they keep a pulse on which students are ready to learn the targets and which need prerequisite support. Often, they take this pulse by analyzing universal screeners, standards-based reports from previous grades, and unit preassessments. The more recent the data, the more relevant it is in teacher decision making. In addition, through regular formative assessment, they keep monitoring who is learning the targets and who needs support. Classroom instruction is then organized to accommodate these needs. These needs are going to occur; not every student learns at the same rate.

Teachers can accommodate these needs through several strategies in Tier 1 instruction. Small-group instruction, while potentially powerful, is targeted and used judiciously. It does not consistently erode time for Tier 1 instruction.

- **Workshops:** Workshops provide opportunities for differentiated grouping to fill prerequisite needs related to the upcoming grade-level learning targets or to reteach targets in which students did not show mastery. While the teacher provides this individual or small-group attention, other students participate in meaningful activities that advance their learning. For example, a teacher may identify six students who need additional instruction for understanding the concept of multiplication. The teacher provides that instruction to this group of students by presenting the concept in a new way, while other students practice independently.
- **Pacing guides that anticipate reteaching:** If teachers anticipate fifteen lessons in a unit, for example, adding two days to the pacing guide is reasonable. This allows them to flexibly use time dedicated for two whole-class instructional lessons or smaller portions of several lesson times to meet the needs of smaller groups of learners.
- **Learning stations:** Teachers design two to four parallel activities for groups of students to complete based on their current performance. All these activities are designed to advance student learning toward grade-level learning or higher while simultaneously addressing particular skills.

Teachers will find the art of understanding when it is best to address individual, small-group, or whole-class needs. Generally, 80 percent class proficiency indicates teachers can drill down into smaller groups and individuals. The greater the percentage of students not demonstrating success on a learning target or showing prerequisite skills, the greater the need to address the whole class and implement new instructional strategies.

This may seem cumbersome or overwhelming. However, keep in mind that the focus is on the learning deemed most essential—not every skill or content objective. In addition, educators achieve greater success (and somewhat ease their burden) when they collaborate to revise their instruction rather than simply reteaching the same way.

Addressing Needs in Tier 2

Tier 2 instruction involves providing additional time and support to meet expected proficiency on essential grade- or course-level standards (Mattos et al., 2024). Educators addressing ongoing needs by modifying their instruction and providing regular reteaching opportunities within units of study may be considered Tier 1 support. A student needing more intensive support to reach grade-level proficiency in an academic or behavioral skill is Tier 2. This instruction is not provided at the expense of initial Tier 1 instruction (Mattos et al., 2024).

Tier 2 supports often come via instructional time specifically identified for this purpose (often called *RTI periods* or *what I need time*), identified small groups in a workshop model, and other designated times for addressing intervention needs. No matter when this occurs, it is critical students do not miss Tier 1 in order to receive this extra time and support. In addition, it is important to remember this is the grade-level or content area teachers' and collaborative teams' responsibility to provide. Because the focus is grade- or course-level standards, it is the classroom teacher's expertise and responsibility. While other staff may be available to support these instructional times, as a team, classroom teachers hold this obligation. Teams should have discussions, by learning target or standard, about the best strategies. To capitalize on the team's expertise and increase the feasibility of this process, the collaborative team can determine the best strategies for this instruction or even share students based on team members' skill sets.

Addressing Needs in Tier 3

Despite everyone's best efforts, some students perform significantly below grade or course level on universal skills such as decoding, comprehension, and number sense. Tier 3 interventions go beyond the support provided in Tier 1 and Tier 2 interventions, which focus on essential standards identified for the grade level or course. Tier 3, rather, focuses on the previously mentioned universal skills that students must develop to achieve learning goals.

While classroom teachers may be involved in serving these needs, generally, staff who have additional training and resources provide this support to students. Examples of those providing interventions can include a trained reading teacher, a teacher who has been trained in mathematics interventions, or a teacher with a specialized expertise in writing. Pending size and structures, many schools may not have staff dedicated full time to these Tier 3 interventions. Therefore, instead, classroom teachers receive training, support, and time to address this system need. Their focus shifts from grade-level standards or immediate prerequisites to intensive reinforcement for universal skills during this identified time (Mattos et al., 2024).

No matter who delivers the intervention, the same Tier 2 instruction concepts are maintained. Students receiving this additional universal skill support must still have access to Tier 1 universal instruction and, in addition, must also be able to access Tier 2 support as needed. Educators can treat that support as a system of safety nets. The school intervention team monitors data, plans interventions, and appropriately monitors those interventions. The school intervention team strives to provide the necessary support so that students become proficient in universal skills at or above grade level, increasing their access to grade-level curriculum.

Discussion Questions and Next Steps Resources

Consider these questions after reading this chapter.

* How does the team support each other in determining and providing interventions?
* When do tiered interventions occur?
* How do we determine who needs additional time and support?

Suggested resources follow that can help you take next steps (if your existing PLC has not yet addressed those elements). These are in addition to the foundational texts mentioned in the introduction.

* William M. Ferriter and colleagues' (2025) *The Big Book of Tools for RTI at Work*
* Jason E. Harlacher and colleagues' (2024) *Untangling Data-Based Decision Making: A Problem-Solving Model to Enhance MTSS*
* Sharon V. Kramer and colleagues' (2020) *Best Practices at Tier 2: Supplemental Interventions for Additional Student Support, Elementary*
* Matt Navo and Amy Williams's (2022) *Demystifying MTSS: A School and District Framework for Meeting Students' Academic and Social-Emotional Needs*
* Paula Rogers and colleagues' (2020) *Best Practices at Tier 3: Intensive Interventions for Remediation, Elementary/Secondary*
* Bob Sonju and colleagues' (2019) *Best Practices at Tier 2: Supplemental Interventions for Additional Student Support, Secondary*

Activities

Before moving on to the activities, ask participants to complete the reproducible "Topic Processing: Critical Question Three" (page 102) to ensure they have a foundational understanding that allows them to apply their learning. Then have participants complete the reproducible "Analyzing the Current Reality: Critical

Question Three" (page 103). It will help you learn the team's implementation and response to that question and determine what may come next for them. To complete this tool, you may need to ask questions of your team and school leadership.

The following activities deepen a participant's understanding of critical question three. As the facilitator, you may choose to use one, some, or all of these learning opportunities based on need. In addition, you can modify any activity to meet adult learners' needs and facilitate engaged learning.

- **Scenarios: Critical Question Three in a PLC at Work** provides an opportunity to reflect on how different teams provide additional time and support. Participants determine what, from each provided scenario, is representative of a collaborative team in a PLC at Work and what is not. Each scenario has elements that are and are not representative, allowing participants to complete the provided graphic organizer and to have a rich discussion based on their analysis. The facilitator, prior to using this activity, can add or modify scenarios to create greater relevance based on the audience.

- **Determining Actions: Planning How to Respond** places participants in a scenario where they have to examine assessment data and plan how to respond. This provides a collaborative learning experience to deepen understanding of how teams respond to data to provide additional time and support to students in need. The ultimate intention is to build confidence in the process so participants can replicate it with collaborative teams using their own assessment data. The provided learning targets can be exchanged with those actually used by participants in order to make the activity more applicable for the audience.

- **Doing the Work: A Reteaching Plan** gives participants the chance to deepen their understanding by developing a reteaching plan that is relevant to them. This more open-ended activity allows participants to choose a standard or target they would actually provide. Whether this activity is conducted individually, in small groups, or in collaborative teams, the facilitator should monitor participant responses (written in the reproducible) throughout and provide feedback and insights. The reproducible also works as a graphic organizer for collaborative teams during their regularly scheduled collaboration to develop reteaching plans.

> *Facilitating Professional Learning*
>
> **Make sure participants know what is next.**
>
> A high-quality professional learning session will offer a follow-up. Let participants know if there will be one, if there is upcoming implementation coaching based on what they learned, or if they will receive future feedback. This does not mean there has to be a post-professional threat for not implementing the learning. It does mean that participants must be clear about what they now must do and their next steps to do so.

Scenarios: Critical Question Three in a PLC at Work

In this activity, participants review scenarios to discuss and identify what parts of the scenario represent understanding of critical question three in a PLC at Work and what parts do not. While some of the scenarios may seem obvious, it is the discussion of *why* that makes this learning activity meaningful.

Follow these steps.

1. Before beginning, ensure some type of professional learning was shared to support the participants' understanding. This may be reading and debriefing this chapter's text.

2. Provide each participant with a copy of "Scenarios: Critical Question Three in a PLC at Work" (page 104) or display for all to read. Keep a copy of "Scenarios: Critical Question Three in a PLC at Work Key" (page 106) for yourself to support discussion.

3. Ensure each participant has a partner or group to engage with. Cap groups at four people to allow effective discussion.

4. One round at a time, have participants read a scenario. Participants then, in the What Is Representative of a PLC and What Is *Not* Representative of a PLC columns, record details from the scenarios accordingly. Ask participants to refrain from moving on to the next round when they are done.

5. After each participant has read the scenario and recorded their rationale, they discuss it with their partner or group. This can include the facilitator checking for consensus on the rationale and engaging in conversation where there may be disagreement. For example, you may ask for participants to share their answer, the rationale for their answer, and doubts about their answer.

6. If there is more than one group of participants, facilitate a whole-group conversation to see if there is consensus or dissonance on the rationale.

7. Provide the group with the answers from "Scenarios: Critical Question Three in a PLC at Work Key" to spur further conversation.

8. Pending the group's answers, further discussion may be needed to provide a deeper understanding of the suggested answers and evidence. For example, if there are significant disagreements or misunderstandings, the facilitator may need to refer to resources on the concept to provide participants additional opportunities to learn.

9. Proceed to subsequent rounds, repeating the process.

Determining Actions: Planning How to Respond

In this activity, participants look at common assessment data for a team of teachers. Based on these data, they discuss how they might proceed to support students in need of additional time and support. While there are some suggested answers, it is most meaningful for participants to think through how they would respond in their setting.

Follow these steps.

1. Before beginning, ensure some type of professional learning was shared to support the participants' understanding. This may be reading and debriefing this chapter's text.

2. Provide each participant with a copy of "Determining Actions: Planning How to Respond" (page 108) or display for all to read. Keep a copy of "Determining Actions: Planning How to Respond Key" (page 109) for yourself to support discussion.

3. Ensure each participant has a partner or group to engage with. Cap groups at four people to allow effective discussion.

4. One round at a time, participants read the learning target and team's data. Then, in the Possible Actions column, they write their suggestions for the team's response to student needs. Ask participants to refrain from moving on to the next round.

5. After each participant has read the scenario and recorded their rationale, they discuss with their partner or group. This can include checking for consensus on their rationale and discussing disagreements.

6. If there is more than one group of participants, facilitate a whole-group conversation to see if there is consensus or dissonance on the rationale.

7. Provide the group with the answers from "Determining Actions: Planning How to Respond Key" to spur further conversation.

8. Pending the group's answers, further discussion may be needed to provide a deeper understanding of the suggested answers and evidence. For example, if there are significant disagreements or misunderstandings, the facilitator may need to refer to resources on the concept to provide participants additional opportunities to learn.

9. Proceed to subsequent rounds, repeating the process.

The facilitator may exchange the listed standards, fitting the site's chosen standards or standards relevant to the participants, to make this activity more relevant to the participants.

Doing the Work: A Reteaching Plan

In this activity, participants reflect on a standard they have recently taught where not all students demonstrated proficiency. Based on this self-selected standard, participants think through how they could respond to student needs. You can facilitate this activity for individuals, groups, or collaborative teams. While it is most beneficial to complete this activity in the actual collaborative team, the process is still meaningful otherwise.

Follow these steps.

1. Before beginning, ensure some type of professional learning was shared to support the participants' understanding. This may be reading and debriefing this chapter's text.

2. Provide each participant with a copy of "Doing the Work: A Reteaching Plan" (page 110) or display for all to read. Keep a copy of "Doing the Work: A Reteaching Plan Key" (page 111) for yourself to support discussion.

3. Participants work through the document's prompts. This can be done individually, in partnerships, or in groups. If the entire collaborative team is present, this is a fitting activity for members to complete together.

4. Facilitate a whole-group conversation. Responses on "Doing the Work: A Reteaching Plan Key" can help guide the discussion. Additional potential whole-group discussion questions follow.

   ▸ What was the most challenging part of this process and why?

   ▸ How can a team approach to this process be beneficial?

   ▸ What are the benefits of a team engaging in this process?

Topic Processing: Critical Question Three

Is this a success area or a growth area for me, my team, or my school, and why?	What are my next steps to grow in my understanding?	Where can I get support to grow?

Propel Your PLC at Work © 2025 Solution Tree Press • SolutionTree.com
Visit **go.SolutionTree.com/PLCbooks** to download this free reproducible.

Analyzing the Current Reality: Critical Question Three

To complete this tool, you may need to ask questions of your team and school leadership. Doing so will assist your understanding and help you learn what may come next for your team. The evidence column allows you to provide specific evidence of the current reality.

Concept	Current Reality	Evidence
My team has a process to identify students in need of additional time and support to achieve essential grade-level learning.	☐ Not at all true. ☐ Somewhat true. ☐ Mostly true. ☐ Always true.	
My team understands instructional strategies to support students who need additional support to learn grade-level standards.	☐ Not at all true. ☐ Somewhat true. ☐ Mostly true. ☐ Always true.	
My team has a process for addressing prerequisite skills.	☐ Not at all true. ☐ Somewhat true. ☐ Mostly true. ☐ Always true.	
My team has a process for reteaching essential learning.	☐ Not at all true. ☐ Somewhat true. ☐ Mostly true. ☐ Always true.	
My team understands how to share concerns about a student who lacks universal skills to a schoolwide team.	☐ Not at all true. ☐ Somewhat true. ☐ Mostly true. ☐ Always true.	

Propel Your PLC at Work © 2025 Solution Tree Press • SolutionTree.com
Visit **go.SolutionTree.com/PLCbooks** to download this free reproducible.

Scenarios: Critical Question Three in a PLC at Work

Scenario	What Is Representative of a PLC at Work	What Is Not Representative of a PLC at Work
Round one A team analyzes a common end-of-unit assessment. They determine which students are not yet proficient in the essential learning for the unit of study. The team decides to provide this list of students to a specialist on-site and asks that they address these students' needs.		
Round two A team creates a list of students who need additional time and support to meet grade-level learning standards based on a common assessment. The team decides the teacher who had the best data will provide small-group instruction for the identified students.		
Round three A team of educators, after analyzing a common assessment, has a list of students who need additional time and support. However, they determine they must move on to the next unit of study and will delay supporting these students.		

Propel Your PLC at Work © 2025 Solution Tree Press • SolutionTree.com
Visit **go.SolutionTree.com/PLCbooks** to download this free reproducible.

Round four A team analyzes a common assessment. The team determines, based on this assessment, who needs additional support. After looking at the list, the team decides the issue with the students on the list is not their instruction. Rather, it is students' attentiveness and motivation to succeed.		
Round five A team uses a common assessment to determine who needs additional time and support on essential learning targets. The team shares strategies they have found successful for reteaching. They also identify times when the learning will occur.		

Scenarios: Critical Question Three in a PLC at Work Key

Scenario	What Is Representative of a PLC	What Is Not Representative of a PLC
Round one A team analyzes a common end-of-unit assessment. They determine which students are not yet proficient in the essential learning for the unit of study. The team decides to provide this list of students to a specialist on-site and asks that they address these students' needs.	The team uses a common assessment to determine who is and is not proficient.	The team is expecting someone else to support the students rather than taking responsibility themselves for reteaching grade-level instruction.
Round two A team creates a list of students who need additional time and support to meet grade-level learning standards based on a common assessment. The team decides the teacher who had the best data will provide small-group instruction for the identified students.	The team uses a common assessment to determine who is not yet proficient. In addition, the team makes a plan for addressing student needs.	The team assigns all students in need of support to one teacher. While sharing students is a valid strategy, it is not sustainable to assign all students in need of support to one teacher. In addition, educators should learn from their peers to advance their own practice.
Round three A team of educators, after analyzing a common assessment, has a list of students who need additional time and support. However, they determine they must move on to the next unit of study and will delay supporting these students.	The team used a common assessment to determine students in need of additional support.	The team did not establish a structure to ensure additional time and support actually occurs. This shows this action is not really a priority for the team.

Propel Your PLC at Work © 2025 Solution Tree Press • SolutionTree.com
Visit **go.SolutionTree.com/PLCbooks** to download this free reproducible.

Round four A team analyzes a common assessment. The team determines, based on this assessment, who needs additional support. After looking at the list, the team decides the issue with the students on the list is not their instruction. Rather, it is students' attentiveness and motivation to succeed.	The team uses a common assessment to determine who needs additional time and support. They also explore why students need that support.	The team does not take ownership of student learning and does not create an actual plan to support students. Instead, they blame students for their outcomes.
Round five A team uses a common assessment to determine who needs additional time and support on essential learning targets. The team shares strategies they have found successful for reteaching. They also identify times when the learning will occur.	This team uses a common assessment to determine who needs additional time and support, shares strategies they believe will be effective, and designates time for the interventions to occur.	While the team identified a time for the intervention to occur, the team will have no real way of knowing how long interventions will take. So, they could consider coming back to this topic for further conversation based on the progress of interventions.

Determining Actions: Planning How to Respond

Learning Target	Team's Data	Possible Actions
Round one **Content Area:** English language arts **Grade Level:** 4 **Standard:** Students can identify the plot of a story.	Teacher A: 16 of 25 students are proficient. Teacher B: 20 of 25 students are proficient. Teacher C: 21 of 25 students are proficient. Teacher D: 18 of 25 students are proficient.	
Round two **Content Area:** Social studies **Grade Level:** 8 **Standard:** Students can state a claim and cite specific evidence from at least two different sources.	Teacher A: 8 of 25 students are proficient. Teacher B: 12 of 25 students are proficient. Teacher C: 14 of 25 students are proficient. Teacher D: 14 of 25 students are proficient.	
Round three **Content Area:** Physical education **Grade Level:** 1 **Standard:** Students can throw a ball at a target and explain the process of throwing.	Teacher A: 23 of 25 students are proficient. Teacher B: 23 of 25 students are proficient. Teacher C: 21 of 25 students are proficient. Teacher D: 10 of 25 students are proficient.	

Determining Actions: Planning How to Respond Key

Learning Target	Team's Data	Possible Actions
Round one Content Area: English language arts Grade Level: 4 Standard: Students can identify the plot of a story.	Teacher A: 16 of 25 students are proficient. Teacher B: 20 of 25 students are proficient. Teacher C: 21 of 25 students are proficient. Teacher D: 18 of 25 students are proficient.	Most of the team has high levels of proficiency. Therefore, the team should look at small-group instruction to reteach the standards. Possible actions could include methods that are different from their original methods of instruction. Teachers B and C may be able to provide insight based on their levels of success.
Round two Content Area: Social studies Grade Level: 8 Standard: Students can state a claim and cite specific evidence from at least two different sources.	Teacher A: 8 of 25 students are proficient. Teacher B: 12 of 25 students are proficient. Teacher C: 14 of 25 students are proficient. Teacher D: 14 of 25 students are proficient.	The team largely has low levels of proficiency. Instead of moving to small-group reteaching, the team should consider reteaching the standard to the whole group. It would benefit the team to discuss how to do this in a different manner as compared to their first strategy. They may consult someone else at their site who may have a skill set that supports the team's learning.
Round three Content Area: Physical education Grade Level: 1 Standard: Students can throw a ball at a target and explain the process of throwing.	Teacher A: 23 of 25 students are proficient. Teacher B: 23 of 25 students are proficient. Teacher C: 21 of 25 students are proficient. Teacher D: 10 of 25 students are proficient.	The team has high levels of proficiency except for teacher D. The team should discuss strategies for intervening and provide teachers A and B the opportunity to share how they reached such high levels of success. In addition, the team could invite teacher D to observe lessons or otherwise provide additional peer support.

Doing the Work: A Reteaching Plan

Question	Answer
What is a standard or learning target you recently taught and noticed many students struggled with?	
Why do you believe students struggled with this standard or target? What was the specific difficulty?	
How was this standard or target initially taught? What instructional strategies were used?	
How could you reteach this standard or target in a different manner to increase proficiency?	
Who could you go to at your site to support your professional practice and help you develop your reteaching plan?	

Propel Your PLC at Work © 2025 Solution Tree Press • SolutionTree.com
Visit **go.SolutionTree.com/PLCbooks** to download this free reproducible.

Doing the Work: A Reteaching Plan Key

Question	Answer
What is a standard or learning target you recently taught and noticed many students struggled with?	Participants should choose a standard they have actual experience with. If participants are new to teaching, are administrators, or are another group of educators who may have a challenging time choosing a standard, the facilitator could provide a relevant one that will be used.
Why do you believe students struggled with this standard or target? What was the specific difficulty?	This is an important step to have participants really think about what part of the standard or target students struggled with, which will inform their response.
How was this standard or target initially taught? What instructional strategies were used?	This is important so that different strategies will be utilized when it comes to reteaching.
How could you reteach this standard or target in a different manner to increase proficiency?	The facilitator can help teams understand that reteaching should be different from the original method of teaching. This may mean introducing manipulatives in mathematics, providing more scaffolds than previously provided, and the like.
Who could you go to at your site to support your professional practice and help you develop your reteaching plan?	This is an important step to support collaboration and use expertise in the building. A teacher from another grade level may be an expert and be able to support. Or, perhaps there is a specialist in the building who can help, such as a special education teacher or reading specialist. The first place a teacher should look is their team, but others can also contribute.

Propel Your PLC at Work © 2025 Solution Tree Press • SolutionTree.com
Visit **go.SolutionTree.com/PLCbooks** to download this free reproducible.

Chapter Seven

Critical Question Four

The first big idea of a PLC is a focus on learning. Schools committed to high levels of learning for all students ensure teachers and teams answer critical question four in a PLC at Work, which asks about students who have already reached proficiency. That does not mean teachers need to provide thirty different lesson plans for thirty different students. It means that, just as they provide interventions for students who need additional time and support, they provide opportunities to *extend* learning for students who are ready to receive them. This can be as simple as creating two or three slightly different learning activities at times or providing fewer scaffolds for those activities.

This chapter deepens the understanding of how teams address the needs of learners who meet proficiency. Content here builds on critical questions one and two of a PLC at Work. As educators gain evidence that students are not proficient in an essential skill, they pursue additional time and support to meet that need. Question four is the other path—addressing the needs of those who have shown proficiency.

Understanding Critical Question Four

Traditionally, schools and teams spend most of their time addressing critical question three of a PLC at Work: "How will we respond when some students do not learn" (DuFour et al., 2024, p. 44)? This is logical. However, they must also ensure their processes embody critical question four: "How will we extend the learning for students who are already proficient" (DuFour et al., 2024, p. 44)? If a school is committed to high levels of learning for every student, this means *also* ensuring students performing at or above grade level grow at least one year's growth in that school year. Therefore, the same process that is applied in question three is applied to question four. First, assessing and responsibility are discussed, then differentiation.

This section is written with the assumption that a collaborative team is formed around teachers who share a common course or content. However, vertical or cross-discipline teams apply the same principles to the learning they are emphasizing as a team.

Assessing and Responsibility

It is significantly easier to determine which students would benefit from extension when teams carefully, collaboratively plan assessments and distinguish proficiency for each target just as they do to identify students in need of additional time and support. Educators can answer question four in different ways depending on their context. Most important is using pre-, interim, and end-of-unit assessments to determine which students are proficient and could benefit from extension opportunities. This occurs at the same time the team screens for students who may need intervention. The assessments that help determine who needs additional time and support can also help determine who can benefit from learning above grade level. No additional assessments are needed.

Teachers and teams ensure the following about students who are proficient.

- **These students do not have more work piled on:** Rather, teachers and teams should consider how their learning path could look *different* from others.

- **Students are not labeled *advanced*:** If we are carefully choosing and assessing essential learning targets, we are likely to have students show the need for intervention in one unit or target and show the need for extension in another. We approach students on a standard-by-standard or skill-by-skill basis.

Providing extension opportunities based on the essential standards and associated learning targets is the collaborative team's responsibility, whether they are a grade-level, content area, or other type of collaborative team. They can deliver extensions when other students are receiving intervention or alter some learning activities in universal instruction to meet these students' needs (some ideas are provided later in this text). However, one example is learning activities or assignments based on varied readiness levels—some students do an activity or assignment with scaffolds (critical question three), some do an assignment for additional practice, and some do an activity that offers additional challenge (critical question four).

However, it is beneficial for the collaborative team to share strategies and co-plan actions just as they would for planning interventions. Teams will likely experience some students who consistently perform at and beyond grade level, demonstrating the need for a more comprehensive plan. In this case, the teachers and team continue addressing extensions on grade-level standards and, additionally, consult the appropriate school team and personnel to help develop a more comprehensive and ongoing plan for the individual student. This may be the school intervention team, site advanced learning personnel, or the guiding coalition.

Differentiation

Extension opportunities for students in a unit are based on essential standards. For example, if a student shows proficiency multiplying single digits, citing evidence in writing, or determining the author's main point in a text (which may all be essential standards), that student doesn't need the same practice as students who are not yet proficient in those skills. However, the currently proficient students can go deeper and beyond the standards' current expectations. This narrows the focus, making the task for educators and teams more doable.

The team, ideally, becomes familiar with differentiation options and some additional professional reading about strategies to extend learning. There is no single strategy, as each content area, learning target, and student may need something a bit different. Over time, teams develop a toolbox with a variety of approaches, and collaboration helps ensure everyone is aware of the tools. Starting with an understanding of what differentiation really is can go a long way for the team. Differentiation allows teacher creativity and endless options. However, the following commonly used strategies—used in a manner that does not erode Tier 1 instruction that benefits all learners—apply across content areas and grade levels.

- **Flexible grouping:** This approach can work in a workshop approach or on reteaching or extension days. Flexible grouping allows a teacher to gather students based on the particular skill they can extend and provide small-group instruction (Weichel, McCann, & Williams, 2018). This group is not stagnant. It is, rather, organized around each target. Each time this group is formed, the student makeup will be different.

- **Tiered assignments:** All students receive an activity or assignment. However, the tasks can be different based on student need (Weichel et al., 2018). For example, there may be three parallel activities in the course. One of those is for students who need a challenge above grade level based on their demonstration of learning. None of the tiered assignments should lead to learning lower than grade level. This strategy is a fairly structured way to use Tomlinson's (2017) concepts of differentiation.

- **Multi-level learning stations:** Students cooperatively learn through tasks or a type of learning center in the classroom. However, the teacher can differentiate the complexity or the scaffolds (Weichel et al., 2018). Again, this is in line with Tomlinson's (2017) concepts of differentiation. Just as with other strategies, teachers ensure the differentiation does not lead to lower than grade-level pathways or detract from high-quality universal instruction that benefits all students.

Educator and author Carol Ann Tomlinson (2017) does a marvelous job of making differentiation doable for educators. She presents the idea that educators can differentiate through content, process, product, and affect (emotions) or environment. This occurs according to the following three things about a student (Tomlinson, 2017).

- **Readiness:** The students' next step that will help them grow their learning
- **Interests:** The areas of study the students would like to pursue or seem to enjoy
- **Learning profile:** The ways students prefer to engage in and process learning

When teams understand this and know what those look like in students, it becomes easier and less time consuming to design learning activities to meet student needs.

Finally, recognize it is not always a student's readiness that needs differentiation. We can support learners through incorporating interests and differing processes, engaging the learners in higher-level cognitive tasks. Be aware of concentrating solely on readiness, or meeting students where they are, which can unintentionally lower rigor and expectations. All students deserve grade-level or higher instruction.

> ### Discussion Questions and Next Steps Resources
>
> **Consider these questions after reading this chapter.**
>
> * Do we take time to identify students who may need extensions? Why or why not?
> * Do we take time to provide extension opportunities for students? Why or why not?
> * Do we have a toolbox of strategies we can use to effectively support extensions? How do we continue developing this toolbox?
>
> Suggested resources follow that can help you take next steps (if your existing PLC has not yet addressed those elements). These are in addition to the foundational texts mentioned in the introduction.
>
> * Kim Bailey and Chris Jakicic's (2018) *Make It Happen: Coaching With the Four Critical Questions of PLCs at Work*
> * Michael Roberts's (2019) *Enriching the Learning: Meaningful Extensions for Proficient Students in a PLC at Work*
> * Carol Ann Tomlinson's (2017) *How to Differentiate Instruction in Academically Diverse Classrooms*, Third Edition
> * Mark Weichel, Blane McCann, and Tami Williams's (2018) *When They Already Know It: How to Extend and Personalize Student Learning in a PLC at Work*

Activities

Before moving on to the activities, ask participants to complete the reproducible "Topic Processing: Critical Question Four" (page 119) to ensure they have a foundational understanding that allows them to apply their learning. Then have participants complete the reproducible "Analyzing the Current Reality: Critical Question Four" (page 120). It helps you learn the team's implementation and response to that question and determine what may come next for them. To complete this tool, you may need to ask questions of your team and school leadership.

The following activities deepen a participant's understanding of critical question four. As the facilitator, you may choose to use one, some, or all of these learning opportunities based on need. In addition, you can modify any activity to meet adult learners' needs and facilitate engaged learning.

- **Scenarios: Critical Question Four in a PLC at Work** allows participants to further their understanding of how collaborative teams in a PLC at Work provide opportunities for learning that go beyond the intended learning goals. Scenarios allow participants to critique how different collaborative teams have responded to the question. Each scenario has strengths and weaknesses, which participants use a graphic organizer to identify. If a facilitator has noticed particular team actions, positive or otherwise, they may be exchanged in this activity to increase relevance to the specific site.

- **Categorizing: Strategies to Support Intervention and Extension** deepens understanding of how collaborative teams respond to students who have met desired proficiency levels while also incorporating concepts of how collaborative teams respond to students in need of extra time and support to meet expectations. Participants analyze a strategy that could be used by a collaborative team. They determine if this strategy would support students in need of additional time and support to meet learning goals, support students who are in need of extension or deepening their learning beyond proficiency, or both, and then provide their rationale. While a graphic organizer is provided, the facilitator should ensure learning goes beyond the use of a graphic organizer and include professional conversations leading to a greater understanding.

- **Doing the Work: An Extension Plan**, like the Doing the Work: A Reteaching Plan activity in chapter 6 (page 101), is more open-ended. This opportunity lets educators practice developing an extension plan that they could actually employ. Teams can also use this tool in support of their own content and data to initiate or refine their processes. Collaborative discussions, no matter how this activity is used, are a critical element if the true goal is deepening understanding.

> ## Facilitating Professional Learning
>
> **Consider what participants will take with them.**
>
> During a professional learning session, you want participants to be focused on the learning. They need to know the what, the why, and the how. However, you do not want them to worry about taking copious notes, recording you speaking, or other ways to capture the learning. Facilitators can focus more on learning in a session when participants are provided handouts, slide decks, or other tools to take with them. At the onset of the learning session, let them know what will be available to them at the conclusion.

Scenarios: Critical Question Four in a PLC at Work

In this activity, participants review scenarios to discuss and identify what parts of the scenario represent an understanding of critical question four in a PLC at Work and what parts do not. While some of the scenarios may seem obvious, it is the discussion of *why* that makes this learning activity meaningful.

Follow these steps.

1. Before beginning, ensure some type of professional learning was shared to support the participants' understanding. This may be reading and debriefing this chapter's text.

2. Provide each participant with a copy of "Scenarios: Critical Question Four in a PLC at Work" (page 121) or display for all to read. Keep a copy of "Scenarios: Critical Question Four in a PLC at Work Key" (page 123) for yourself to support discussion.

3. Ensure each participant has a partner or group to engage with. Cap groups at four people to allow effective discussion.

4. One round at a time, have participants read a scenario. Participants then, in the What Is Representative of a PLC and What Is *Not* Representative of a PLC columns, record details from the scenarios accordingly. Ask participants to refrain from moving on to the next round when they are done.

5. After each participant has read the scenario and recorded their rationale, they discuss with their partner or group. This can include the facilitator checking for consensus on the rationale and engaging in conversation where there may be disagreement. For example, you may ask for participants to share their answer, the rationale for their answer, and doubts about their answer.

6. If there is more than one group of participants, facilitate a whole-group conversation to see if there is consensus or dissonance on the rationale.

7. Provide the group with the answers from "Scenarios: Critical Question Four in a PLC at Work Key" to spur further conversation.

8. Pending the group's answers, further discussion may be needed to provide a deeper understanding of the suggested answers and evidence. For example, if there are significant disagreements or misunderstandings, the facilitator may need to refer to resources on the concept to provide participants additional opportunities to learn.

9. Proceed to subsequent rounds, repeating the process.

Categorizing: Strategies to Support Intervention and Extension

In this activity, participants review different strategies that teachers may use to support critical questions three and four. This provides general strategies to support learning, adding to their instructional toolbox.

Follow these steps.

1. Before beginning, ensure some type of professional learning was shared to support the participants' understanding. This may be reading and debriefing this chapter's text.

2. Provide each participant with a copy of "Categorizing: Strategies to Support Intervention and Extension" (page 125) or display for all to read. Keep a copy of "Categorizing: Strategies to Support Intervention and Extension Key" (page 127) for yourself to support discussion.

3. Ensure each participant has a partner or group to engage with. Cap groups at four people to allow effective discussion.

4. Have each participant read the strategy in the first column. In the Based on My Knowledge, It Fits Best Here column, they choose either "Supporting students in need of additional time and support" or "Supporting students in need of extension for deepening their learning beyond proficiency." Depending on the strategy, they may select both.

5. After each participant has read the scenario and recorded their rationale, they discuss with their partner or group. This can include checking for consensus on their rationale and discussing disagreements.

6. If there is more than one group of participants, facilitate a whole-group conversation to see if there is consensus or dissonance on the rationale.

7. Provide the group with the answers from "Categorizing: Strategies to Support Intervention and Extension Key" to solidify understanding.

8. Create an opportunity for discussion based on provided answers in order to dialogue, reflect, and come to a unified understanding

Doing the Work: An Extension Plan

In this activity, participants will reflect on a standard they have recently taught and noticed there were students who demonstrated proficiency. Based on this self-selected standard, they think through how they could respond to student needs. This activity can be done individually, in groups, or in collaborative teams. While it is most beneficial to complete this activity in the actual collaborative team, the process is still meaningful for other groups to develop an understanding.

Follow these steps.

1. Before beginning, ensure some type of professional learning was shared to support the participants' understanding. This may be reading and debriefing this chapter's text.

2. Provide each participant with a copy of "Doing the Work: An Extension Plan" (page 129) or display for all to read. Keep a copy of "Doing the Work: An Extension Plan Key" (page 130) for yourself to support discussion.

3. Ensure each participant has a partner or group to engage with. Cap groups at four people to allow effective discussion.

4. Participants should work through the handout.

5. Facilitate a whole-group conversation. Responses from "Doing the Work: An Extension Plan Key" can help guide the discussion. Potential whole-group discussion questions follow.

   ▸ What was the most challenging part of this process and why?

   ▸ How can a team approach to this process be beneficial?

   ▸ What are the benefits of a team engaging in this process?

Topic Processing: Critical Question Four

Is this a success area or a growth area for me, my team, or my school, and why?	What are my next steps to grow in my understanding?	Where can I get support to grow?

Analyzing the Current Reality: Critical Question Four

To complete this tool, you may need to ask questions of your team and school leadership. Doing so will assist your understanding and help you learn what may come next for your team. The evidence column allows you to provide specific evidence of the current reality.

Concept	Current Reality	Evidence
My team has a process to identify students in need of learning extensions.	☐ Not at all true. ☐ Somewhat true. ☐ Mostly true. ☐ Always true.	
My team understands instructional strategies to support students who need additional support or learning extensions.	☐ Not at all true. ☐ Somewhat true. ☐ Mostly true. ☐ Always true.	
My team has a process for pre-screening students who may benefit from alternative learning pathways in a unit of study.	☐ Not at all true. ☐ Somewhat true. ☐ Mostly true. ☐ Always true.	
My team has a process for providing extended learning opportunities.	☐ Not at all true. ☐ Somewhat true. ☐ Mostly true. ☐ Always true.	
My team understands how to seek support for students who may be consistently performing above grade-level expectations.	☐ Not at all true. ☐ Somewhat true. ☐ Mostly true. ☐ Always true.	

Propel Your PLC at Work © 2025 Solution Tree Press • SolutionTree.com
Visit **go.SolutionTree.com/PLCbooks** to download this free reproducible.

Scenarios: Critical Question Four in a PLC at Work

Scenario	What Is Representative of a PLC at Work	What Is Not Representative of a PLC at Work
Round one A team analyzes a common assessment and develops a plan for students who have not yet met proficiency on a standard. While the teacher is working with those students, those students who have demonstrated proficiency will receive free time.		
Round two After analyzing a common assessment, the team decides to group students based on specific needs. One teacher will work with students who need support in the most basic skills of the standard, one teacher will work with students who need support in higher level skills of the standard, and one will work with students who have already demonstrated proficiency.		
Round three A team analyzes an assessment and makes a plan to serve those students who have shown proficiency. During the time where teachers will work with students to intervene and extend, students who have shown proficiency will have the option of completing another worksheet similar to ones they have done, assisting others who need support, or applying their learning to a real-world scenario.		

Round four The teacher has been teaching the subject for many years. Based on his knowledge of students in class and how they have generally been performing, he organizes three groups in his class for an intervention and extension day. One group will meet with him for extra support, one will receive extra practice after viewing a reteaching video, and one will complete a challenge project in a small group.		
Round five A team analyzes assessment data and determines, for the assessed skill, each student who has achieved proficiency. They then reflect on how they can redesign the unit to offer opportunities to proficient learners when they teach the unit next year.		

Scenarios: Critical Question Four in a PLC at Work Key

Scenario	What Is Representative of a PLC at Work	What Is Not Representative of a PLC at Work
Round one A team analyzes a common assessment and develops a plan for students who have not yet met proficiency on a standard. While the teacher is working with those students, those students who have demonstrated proficiency will receive free time.	The team analyzes an assessment and knows who is and who is not proficient.	Instead of supporting students who have demonstrated proficiency, the team is only focused on those who have not yet met the standard.
Round two After analyzing a common assessment, the team decides to group students based on specific needs. One teacher will work with students who need support in the most basic skills of the standard, one teacher will work with students who need support in higher level skills of the standard, and one will work with students who have already demonstrated proficiency.	The team analyzes an assessment and devises a plan to meet all student needs.	While it may just be missing from the scenario, we do not see evidence that the team also shared strategies to build the skills of the teachers for future instruction.
Round three A team analyzes an assessment and makes a plan to serve those students who have shown proficiency. During the time where teachers will work with students to intervene and extend, students who have shown proficiency will have the option of completing another worksheet similar to ones they have done, assisting others who need support, or applying their learning to a real-world scenario.	The team has analyzed an assessment and planned for students who have demonstrated proficiency. In addition, they have provided choices for students.	While choice was offered, not all of the choices are likely to be meaningful and lead to deeper levels of learning.

Round four The teacher has been teaching the subject for many years. Based on his knowledge of students in class and how they have generally been performing, he organizes three groups in his class for an intervention and extension day. One group will meet with him for extra support, one will receive extra practice after viewing a reteaching video, and one will complete a challenge project in a small group.	The teacher has organized students and planned activities to support learning.	The teacher does not seem to use collaboration to inform next steps. In addition, the teacher appears to be using his "feelings" versus actual assessment data or observations.
Round five A team analyzes assessment data and determines, for the assessed skill, each student who has achieved proficiency. They then reflect on how they can redesign the unit to offer opportunities to proficient learners when they teach the unit next year.	The team analyzes an assessment and identifies who is proficient. In addition, the team engages in a conversation about bettering adult practice.	The team does not plan to extend the learning for students currently identified as proficient. They have, instead, focused on a change of practice for the following year.

Categorizing: Strategies to Support Intervention and Extension

Strategy	Based on My Knowledge, It Fits Best Here	Rationale
Round one Additional application: Design a prompt that will provide an opportunity for students to take what they know and apply it to a new situation that is likely at a higher level of thinking. This may be a real-world situation, cross-discipline situation, or a situation of the student's choice.	☐ Supporting students in need of additional time and support. ☐ Supporting students in need of extension or deepening their learning beyond proficiency.	
Round two Tiered assignments: Design assignments or activities that pursue the same learning goal. However, tailor the activity for different levels of understanding. The teacher may prepare two or three activities that offer different levels of scaffolds (Heacox, 2002).	☐ Supporting students in need of additional time and support. ☐ Supporting students in need of extension or deepening their learning beyond proficiency.	
Round three Scaffolded reteaching: Conduct a small group that reteaches a concept or target in a manner that was not taught before. This may include additional instructional scaffolds like manipulatives, graphic organizers, or more explicit modeling.	☐ Supporting students in need of additional time and support. ☐ Supporting students in need of extension or deepening their learning beyond proficiency.	

Round four Standard advancement: Design an activity for a group of students to achieve the rigor of a similar standard for the grade or grade band above where students are currently assigned.	☐ Supporting students in need of additional time and support. ☐ Supporting students in need of extension or deepening their learning beyond proficiency.	
Round five Additional practice: Design an activity that provides students with the opportunity to practice a taught skill at the same level of rigor as the standard demands.	☐ Supporting students in need of additional time and support. ☐ Supporting students in need of extension or deepening their learning beyond proficiency.	

Heacox, D. (2002). Differentiating instruction in the regular classroom: How to reach and teach all learners, grades 3–12. Minneapolis, MN: Free Spirit.

Categorizing: Strategies to Support Intervention and Extension Key

Strategy	Based on My Knowledge, It Fits Best Here	Rationale
Round one Additional application: Design a prompt that will provide an opportunity for students to take what they know and apply it to a new situation that is likely at a higher level of thinking. This may be a real-world situation, cross-discipline situation, or a situation of the student's choice.	☐ Supporting students in need of additional time and support. ☑ Supporting students who are in need of extension or deepening their learning beyond proficiency.	This strategy provides students the opportunity to bring their learning to a deeper level by applying it to a new area (situation or discipline).
Round two Tiered assignments: Design assignments or activities that pursue the same learning goal. However, tailor the activity for different levels of understanding. The teacher may prepare two or three activities that offer different levels of scaffolds (Heacox, 2002).	☑ Supporting students in need of additional time and support. ☑ Supporting students in need of extension or deepening their learning beyond proficiency.	This strategy supports all students as it pursues a rigorous goal through pathways that have various scaffolds.
Round three Scaffolded reteaching: Conduct a small group that reteaches a concept or target in a manner that was not taught before. This may include additional instructional scaffolds like manipulatives, graphic organizers, or more explicit modeling.	☑ Supporting students in need of additional time and support. ☐ Supporting students in need of extension or deepening their learning beyond proficiency.	This strategy meets the needs of learners who need additional scaffolds to develop the grade-level skill.

Round four Standard advancement: Design an activity for a group of students to achieve the rigor of a similar standard for the grade or grade band above where students are currently assigned.	☐ Supporting students in need of additional time and support. ☑ Supporting students in need of extension or deepening their learning beyond proficiency.	This strategy applies best to students who have shown proficiency in a skill because students are participating in an activity that goes beyond the grade-level expectation.
Round five Additional practice: Design an activity that provides students with the opportunity to practice a taught skill at the same level of rigor as the standard demands.	☑ Supporting students in need of additional time and support. ☐ Supporting students in need of extension or deepening their learning beyond proficiency.	This strategy does not go beyond the expected complexity. If this activity were to be used, it would be best for students who have demonstrated the skill but need additional practice to make it automatic or more solid.

Heacox, D. (2002). Differentiating instruction in the regular classroom: How to reach and teach all learners, grades 3–12. Minneapolis, MN: Free Spirit.

Doing the Work: An Extension Plan

Question	Answer
What is a standard or learning target you recently taught and noticed many students demonstrated proficiency?	
Why do you believe students excelled in this standard or target? What were the specific elements they excelled at?	
What would be a logical next step for this standard, learning target, or raise in rigor for the expectation of learning?	
Based on the logical next step or raise in rigor, how could you facilitate this learning?	
Who could you go to at your sight to support your professional practice and help you develop your extension plan?	

Doing the Work: An Extension Plan Key

Question	Answer
What is a standard or learning target you recently taught and noticed many students demonstrated proficiency?	Participants should choose a standard with which they have actual experience. If participants are new to teaching, are administrators, or another group of educators who may have a challenging time choosing a standard, the facilitator could provide a relevant one to use.
Why do you believe students excelled in this standard or target? What were the specific elements they excelled at?	This is an important step to have participants really think about what part of the standard or target students excelled at so they can incorporate this in their response.
What would be a logical next step for this standard, learning target, or raise in rigor for the expectation of learning?	This is important so that, when it comes to providing an extension, the participants know what the focus should be.
Based on the logical next step or raise in rigor, how could you facilitate this learning?	The facilitator can help teams understand that extension means providing learning opportunities at a higher complexity. It does not mean simply providing more work for a student.
Who could you go to at your sight to support your professional practice and help you develop your extension plan?	This is an important step to support collaboration and use expertise in the building. A teacher from another grade level may be highly skilled and able to support. Or, perhaps there is a specialist in the building that can help. The first place a teacher should look to is their team, but others can also contribute.

Chapter Eight

Teaching-Assessing-Learning Cycle

The teaching-assessing-learning cycle puts the four critical questions of a PLC at Work into an iterative process for a team to follow. *This process ensures learning for students and for teachers.* Students are closely monitored for success and receive additional time and support as needed. Students also receive extension opportunities as needed. Educators are not left out of the learning process as they collaborate with peers to hone their instructional skills and continually work to better their universal Tier 1 instruction. By putting the four critical questions of a PLC into an ongoing process, the teaching-assessing-learning cycle ensures schools are centered on the three big ideas of a PLC. Learning is the focus, learning is achieved through collaboration, and results are monitored to ensure all students achieve at high levels. In this way, if educators are vulnerable and embrace this process, they will achieve at higher levels.

This chapter provides participants the opportunity to learn more about how teams use the teaching-assessing-learning cycle in a PLC at Work. Teams use this method to actualize the four critical questions of a PLC at Work. This chapter can be thought of as the chapter that ties together all the work collaborative teams do to answer the four critical questions.

Understanding the Teaching-Assessing-Learning Cycle

The four critical questions of a PLC are not independent tasks or concepts. Rather, schools should address them as a part of a process. The cycle ties the questions together in a coherent process for teams to utilize. For example, we determine essential standards (critical question one) and use those to develop assessments in our units (critical question two) using the results of the assessments to determine interventions (critical question three) and extensions (critical question four).

The teaching-assessing-learning cycle, through the lens of a collaborative team delivering a unit of study, involves determining the unit's learning goals, intermittently and finally measuring learning in relation to those goals, revising their instructional approach based on data, and addressing intervention and extension needs as a part of the process. This text provides an overview of how teams can implement the teaching-assessing-learning cycle—in pre-, during-, and end-of-unit steps—and is based on *Taking Action*, Second Edition (Mattos et al., 2024) with slight modifications for alignment to this text.

Note that this section assumes a collaborative team is formed around teachers who share a common course or content. However, vertical or cross-discipline teams apply the same principles to the learning they emphasize as a team in learning cycles.

Pre-Unit Steps

The cycle begins before a unit of study. Without that preparation, key ingredients will not guide instruction. As mentioned, teams determine the essential standards and associated learning targets within a unit (which relates to critical question one). This determination then drives the end-of-unit assessment creation (which relates to critical question two). End-of-unit assessments, as with any assessment, are designed to ensure educators and students can identify whether students are proficient or need further support to get there (which relates to critical questions three and four). With the essentials determined and the assessment planned, the unit will have a clear focus.

Additionally, teams plan an appropriate number of interim assessments. These are portions of the end-of-unit or end-of-cycle assessments that measure progress along the way. These provide the chance to check for understanding and react accordingly in short cycles, allowing teachers and teams to quickly respond with interventions and extensions. All of this helps teams determine appropriate pacing for the unit, which must accommodate data reactions. Plan some extra time so teachers can take action based on what they learn from interim assessments.

In-Unit Steps

As teachers and teams execute the instruction of the unit, closely aligned to the chosen essential standards and targets, they closely monitor student performance. This is done through the planned, interim, team-based *common formative assessments* (and sometimes, *CFAs*). In addition, each teacher is likely to provide further assessments to inform their instruction. Both assessments are necessary, but the individual teacher will implement more interim assessments than the team commonly plans and analyzes.

As results of the assessments are analyzed target by target, teachers must react and take action to provide additional time and support for students who have not met expected learning goals. For assessments that were planned by the team, the team analyzes the data together. The collaborative team can then make appropriate plans and share strategies to meet student learning needs. In addition, students showing proficiency have their needs met because the team also plans opportunities for them to deepen or extend their learning. Note that these activities *deepen* or *extend* learning; they do not simply mean more work. It is different work that stretches their learning. The critical focus during a unit of study is using the best instructional strategies known, regularly analyzing student learning, and reteaching or extending essential learning as necessary.

End-of-Unit Steps

As a unit nears the end of the planned pacing, teachers deliver an end-of-unit assessment. For educators, the goal of this assessment is to achieve an extremely high demonstration of learning for all students. After all, the assessment was planned before the unit began, instruction was designed to promote success, and there were multiple checks for learning with intervention along the way.

However, when teachers have some students who need additional time and support and instruction must move on, those students receive Tier 2 intervention support while continuing to receive Tier 1 instruction in the next unit of study. This additional support does not mimic what students received before; the teacher uses new instructional methods. A team can share strategies and, perhaps, group students effectively to work together in addressing these needs. In addition to analyzing student data and providing necessary support, teams reflect on the overall unit of study. They note how what they learned in *this* unit of study impacts instruction in their *next* unit of study and when they revisit this unit in the *following year*. See figure 8.1 for an illustration of this process.

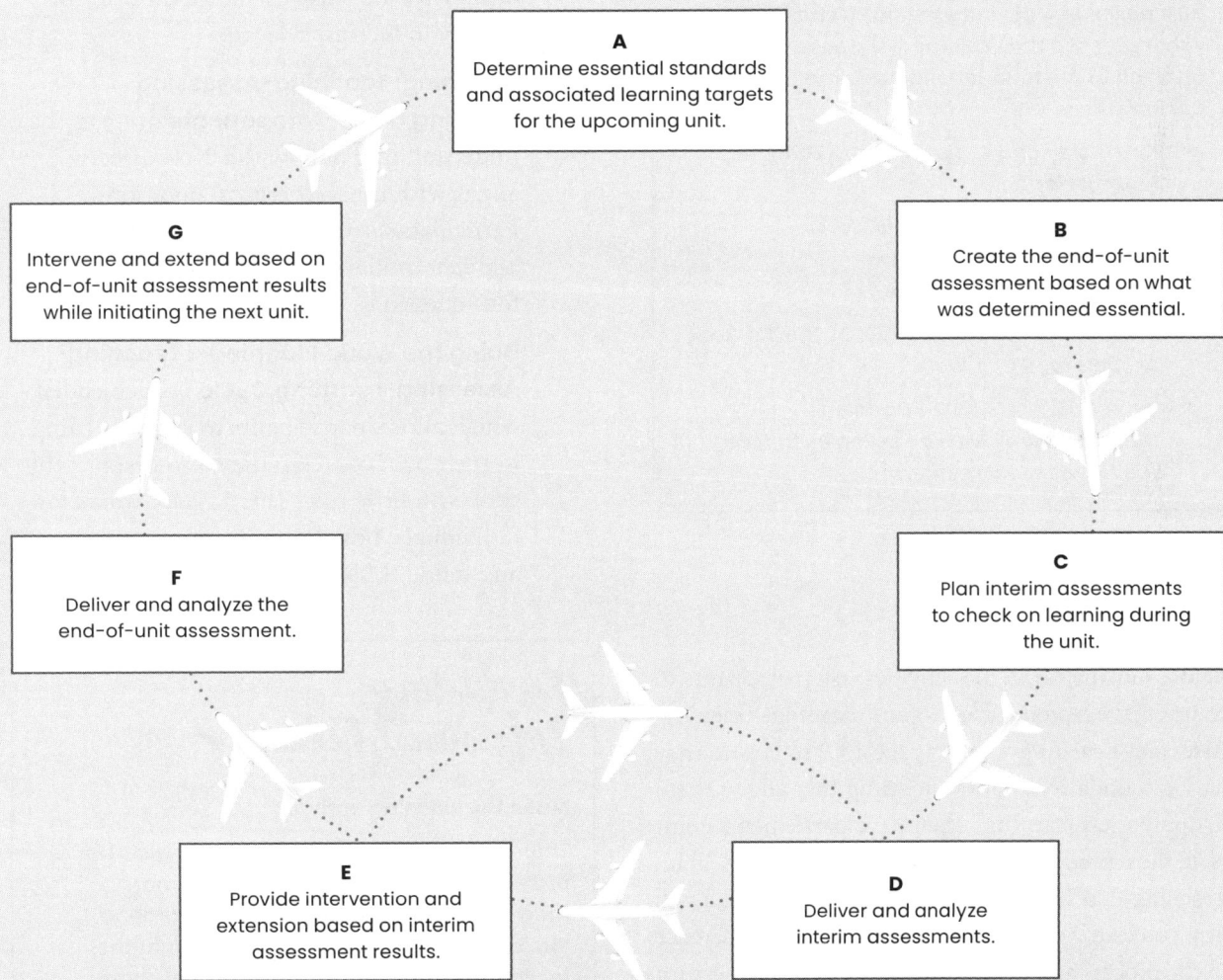

Source: Adapted from Buffum, Mattos, & Weber, 2012; Mattos et al., 2024.

Figure 8.1: Teaching-assessing-learning cycle components.

Discussion Questions and Next Steps Resources

Consider these questions after reading this chapter.

* Is the team efficient at planning the unit of study before we begin instruction? Why or why not?
* What is the team's method to create, deliver, and analyze assessments in a timely manner? Is this effective? Why or why not?
* How does the team help each other when it comes to reteaching when students do not meet proficiency or when students need advanced learning opportunities?

Suggested resources follow that can help you take next steps (if your existing PLC has not yet addressed those elements). These are in addition to the foundational texts mentioned in the introduction.

* Kim Bailey and Chris Jakicic's (2018) *Make It Happen*
* Kim Bailey and Chris Jakicic's (2023) *Common Formative Assessment,* Second Edition
* Ferriter and colleagues' (2025) *The Big Book of Tools for RTI at Work*
* Jane A. G. Kise's (2021) *Doable Differentiation: Twelve Strategies to Meet the Needs of All Learners*

The following activities deepen a participant's understanding of the teaching-assessing-learning cycle. As the facilitator, you may choose to use one, some, or all of these learning opportunities based on need. In addition, you can modify any activity to meet adult learners' needs and facilitate engaged learning.

- **Scenarios: Teaching-Assessing-Learning Cycle** allows participants to further their understanding of how the four critical questions of a PLC operate in a cohesive cycle. Scenarios invite critique about how different collaborative teams implement the cycle. Each scenario has strengths and weaknesses, which participants use a graphic organizer to identify. If the facilitator has noticed particular team actions, positive or otherwise, they may exchange those in this activity to increase relevance.

- **Matching: Teaching-Assessing-Learning Cycle Components** deepens the understanding of how the cycle directly aligns with the four critical questions. Participants, step by step, look at the cycle and determine alignment to each of the four questions.

- **Doing the Work: Planning a Teaching-Assessing-Learning Cycle** is open ended, which allows participants to apply learning to their own context. They also practice this skill with little risk. This activity works for individuals, but also for a team to practice and refine skills.

Activities

Before moving on to the activities, ask participants to complete the reproducible "Topic Processing: Teaching-Assessing-Learning Cycle" (page 139) to ensure they have a foundational understanding that allows them to apply their learning. Then have participants complete the reproducible "Analyzing the Current Reality: Teaching-Assessing-Learning Cycle" (page 140). It will help you learn the team's understanding and adherence to the process and determine what may come next for them. To complete this tool, you may need to ask questions of your team and school leadership.

Facilitating Professional Learning

Make the learning active.

There is no replacement for designing active professional learning time. *Active* is more than having people up and moving around. While that is absolutely beneficial, what the facilitator asks participants to do when they are up and moving around is more important. Mesh what you want participants to know with collaborative opportunities for them to process the information and plan how to use it.

Scenarios: Teaching-Assessing-Learning Cycle

In this activity, participants review scenarios to discuss and identify what parts of the scenario represent the teaching-assessing-learning cycle and what parts do not. While some of the scenarios may seem obvious, it is the discussion of *why* that makes this learning activity meaningful.

Follow these steps.

1. Before beginning, ensure some type of professional learning was shared to support the participants' understanding. This may be reading and debriefing this chapter's text.

2. Provide each participant with a copy of "Scenarios: Teaching-Assessing-Learning Cycle" (page 142) or display for all to read. Keep a copy of "Scenarios: Teaching-Assessing-Learning Cycle Key" (page 144) for yourself to support discussion.

3. Ensure each participant has a partner or group to engage with. Cap groups at four people to allow effective discussion.

4. One round at a time, have participants read a scenario. Participants then, in the What Is Representative of a PLC and What Is *Not* Representative of a PLC columns, record details from the scenarios accordingly. Ask participants to refrain from moving on to the next round when they are done.

5. After each participant has read the scenario and recorded their rationale, they discuss with their partner or group. This can include the facilitator checking for consensus on the rationale and engaging in conversation where there may be disagreement. For example, you may ask for participants to share their answer, the rationale for their answer, and doubts about their answer.

6. If there is more than one group of participants, facilitate a whole-group conversation to see if there is consensus or dissonance on the rationale.

7. Provide the group with the answers from "Scenarios: Teaching-Assessing-Learning Cycle Key" to spur further conversation.

8. Pending the group's answers, further discussion may be needed to provide a deeper understanding of the suggested answers and evidence. For example, if there are significant disagreements or misunderstandings, the facilitator may need to refer to resources on the concept to provide participants additional opportunities to learn.

9. Proceed to subsequent rounds, repeating the process.

Matching: Teaching-Assessing-Learning Cycle Components

This activity helps participants understand how the teaching-assessing-learning cycle is the four critical questions of a PLC in action. While this activity will develop an understanding of the cycle, it will also deepen understanding of the four critical questions. Some participants may debate the alignment of components to questions. For example, some people may consider assessment analysis part of critical question two, and others may align it to critical questions three and four. This is OK; it means participants are thinking critically about the cycle and the work of collaborative teams.

Follow these steps.

1. Before beginning, ensure some type of professional learning was shared to support the participants' understanding. This may be reading and debriefing this chapter's text.

2. Provide each participant with a copy of "Matching: Teaching-Assessing-Learning Cycle Components" (page 146) or display for all to read. Keep a copy of "Matching: Teaching-Assessing-Learning Cycle Components Key" (page 148) for yourself to support discussion.

3. Ensure each participant has a partner or group to engage with. Cap groups at four people to allow effective discussion.

4. Participants match each entry in the Component column to one of the critical questions in the To Which Question This Component Applies column.

5. After each participant has finished matching, they discuss with a partner or group.

6. If there is more than one group of participants, facilitate a whole-group conversation to see if there is consensus or dissonance on the rationale. This can include checking for consensus on their rationale and discussing disagreements.

7. Provide the group with the answers from "Matching: Teaching-Assessing-Learning Cycle Key" to spur further conversation.

8. Pending the group's answers, further discussion may be needed to provide a deeper understanding of the suggested answers and evidence. For example, if there are significant disagreements or misunderstandings, the facilitator may need to refer to resources on the concept to provide participants additional opportunities to learn.

Doing the Work: Planning a Teaching-Assessing-Learning Cycle

In this activity, participants think about an upcoming unit of study or learning cycle. Based on this self-selected unit or cycle, they will think through how they could plan for a teaching-assessing-learning cycle. Participants can do this activity individually, in groups, or in collaborative teams. While it is most beneficial to complete this activity among an actual collaborative team, the process is still meaningful.

Follow these steps.

1. Before beginning, ensure some type of professional learning was shared to support the participants' understanding. This may be reading and debriefing this chapter's text.

2. Provide each participant with a copy of "Doing the Work: Planning a Teaching-Assessing-Learning Cycle" (page 150) or display for all to read. Keep a copy of "Doing the Work: Planning a Teaching-Assessing-Learning Cycle Key" (page 152) for yourself to support discussion.

3. Participants should work through the handout.

4. No matter how the activity was completed, the facilitator should facilitate a conversation that allows for a sharing of ideas to benefit the group as a whole.

Topic Processing:
Teaching-Assessing-Learning Cycle

Is this a success area or a growth area for me, my team, or my school, and why?	What are my next steps to grow in my understanding?	Where can I get support to grow?

Propel Your PLC at Work © 2025 Solution Tree Press • SolutionTree.com
Visit **go.SolutionTree.com/PLCbooks** to download this free reproducible.

Analyzing the Current Reality: Teaching-Assessing-Learning Cycle

To complete this tool, you may need to ask questions of your team and school leadership. Doing so will assist your understanding and help you learn what may come next for your team. The evidence column allows you to provide specific evidence of the current reality.

Concept	Current Reality	Evidence
The team takes intentional steps to plan for an upcoming unit of study. This includes determining essential learning, creating the end-of-unit assessment, and determining pacing for the unit.	☐ Not at all true. ☐ Somewhat true. ☐ Mostly true. ☐ Always true.	
The team takes intentional steps to provide first best instruction, monitor student success, and address needs as they arise.	☐ Not at all true. ☐ Somewhat true. ☐ Mostly true. ☐ Always true.	
The team provides frequent interim assessments on essential skills leading to the end-of-unit assessment and analyzes the results data to impact instruction and address student needs.	☐ Not at all true. ☐ Somewhat true. ☐ Mostly true. ☐ Always true.	

The team provides an end-of-unit assessment and analyzes the results data to impact instruction and address student needs.	☐ Not at all true. ☐ Somewhat true. ☐ Mostly true. ☐ Always true.	
The team reflects on the unit with specific attention on how they used assessment data to inform their instruction and address student needs.	☐ Not at all true. ☐ Somewhat true. ☐ Mostly true. ☐ Always true.	

Scenarios: Teaching-Assessing-Learning Cycle

Scenario	What Is Representative of a PLC at Work	What Is Not Representative of a PLC at Work
Round one A team meets weekly. As a part of their ongoing work, they have developed essential standards for the course they all teach in common. In addition, they have determined a common definition of proficiency for each standard. On a weekly basis, in their meetings, the team discusses which activities they can use to help students learn the essential standards.		
Round two At a team meeting, the team analyzes an end-of-unit assessment. They share their lists of students who are and are not proficient. Based on this, those with the highest levels of proficiency share their instructional approaches that led to those high levels of learning. The team makes notes to use these next year and then turns their attention to the next unit.		
Round three A team meets to share their data based on a common interim assessment within a unit of study. They determine which students are and are not proficient. The team discusses when they will be able to provide reteaching for those who need it, and they also discuss what they feel are the best methods to use to support those identified students.		

Round four At a collaborative team meeting, a member suggests the team should deliver a common interim assessment the next week to check student progress. The team debates what they could assess in common, determines a common learning target, and then plans an exit ticket to measure learning.		
Round five A collaborative team has aligned their essential standards to their units of study. In addition, they have established common end-of-unit assessments. They analyze these assessments together and plan how to address student needs in intervention and extension. The units of study are usually six weeks long.		

Scenarios: Teaching-Assessing-Learning Cycle Key

Scenario	What Is Representative of a PLC at Work?	What Is Not Representative of a PLC at Work?
Round one A team meets weekly. As a part of their ongoing work, they have developed essential standards for the course they all teach in common. In addition, they have determined a common definition of proficiency for each standard. On a weekly basis, in their meetings, the team discusses which activities they can use to help students learn the essential standards.	The team has determined essential standards and developed common proficiency goals. In addition, the team meets weekly.	The team focuses on activities rather than on the elements of the teaching-assessing cycle.
Round two At a team meeting, the team analyzes an end-of-unit assessment. They share their lists of students who are and are not proficient. Based on this, those with the highest levels of proficiency share their instructional approaches that led to those high levels of learning. The team makes notes to use these next year and then turns their attention to the next unit.	The team has delivered a common assessment, analyzed data, and shared effective instructional strategies.	While the team determined who is and is not proficient for the unit of study, they did not make a plan to address student needs.
Round three A team meets to share their data based on a common interim assessment within a unit of study. They determine which students are and are not proficient. The team discusses when they will be able to provide reteaching for those who need it, and they also discuss what they feel are the best methods to use to support those identified students.	The team has delivered a common interim assessment and analyzed data. In addition, they have developed a plan, including time and instructional strategies, to support students who have not met learning goals.	The team planned for those who did not meet learning goals but did not make a plan to support those already demonstrating proficiency. This could mean those students sit idle in identified intervention time.

Round four At a collaborative team meeting, a member suggests the team should deliver a common interim assessment the next week to check student progress. The team debates what they could assess in common, determines a common learning target, and then plans an exit ticket to measure learning.	This team has established a common learning goal and then plans an assessment they will all use.	It is evident that this team is dabbling in the work of a collaborative team and does not utilize the teaching-assessing-learning cycle as intended.
Round five A collaborative team has aligned their essential standards to their units of study. In addition, they have established common end-of-unit assessments. They analyze these assessments together and plan how to address student needs in intervention and extension. The units of study are usually six weeks long.	The team has established essential learning goals and common assessments and meets to plan to support students for both intervention and extension.	It isn't clear if the team discusses instructional practice as a part of their protocol. In addition, the team does not appear to use any common interim assessments in what seems to be rather lengthy units of study.

Matching: Teaching-Assessing-Learning Cycle Components

Check all that apply.

Component	To Which Question This Component Applies and Why (DuFour et al., 2024, p. 44)
Determine essential standards and associated learning targets for the upcoming unit of study.	☐ "What knowledge, skills, and dispositions should every student acquire as a result of this unit, this course, or this grade level?" ☐ "How will we know when each student has acquired the essential knowledge and skills?" ☐ "How will we respond when some students do not learn?" ☐ "How will we extend the learning for students who are already proficient?"
Create the end-of-unit assessment based on what has been determined to be essential.	☐ "What knowledge, skills, and dispositions should every student acquire as a result of this unit, this course, or this grade level?" ☐ "How will we know when each student has acquired the essential knowledge and skills?" ☐ "How will we respond when some students do not learn?" ☐ "How will we extend the learning for students who are already proficient?"
Plan interim assessments that will be used to check on learning within the unit.	☐ "What knowledge, skills, and dispositions should every student acquire as a result of this unit, this course, or this grade level?" ☐ "How will we know when each student has acquired the essential knowledge and skills?" ☐ "How will we respond when some students do not learn?" ☐ "How will we extend the learning for students who are already proficient?"
Deliver and analyze interim assessments.	☐ "What knowledge, skills, and dispositions should every student acquire as a result of this unit, this course, or this grade level?" ☐ "How will we know when each student has acquired the essential knowledge and skills?" ☐ "How will we respond when some students do not learn?" ☐ "How will we extend the learning for students who are already proficient?"

Provide intervention and extension based on the results of interim assessments.	☐ "What knowledge, skills, and dispositions should every student acquire as a result of this unit, this course, or this grade level?" ☐ "How will we know when each student has acquired the essential knowledge and skills?" ☐ "How will we respond when some students do not learn?" ☐ "How will we extend the learning for students who are already proficient?"	
Deliver and analyze the end-of-unit assessment.	☐ "What knowledge, skills, and dispositions should every student acquire as a result of this unit, this course, or this grade level?" ☐ "How will we know when each student has acquired the essential knowledge and skills?" ☐ "How will we respond when some students do not learn?" ☐ "How will we extend the learning for students who are already proficient?"	
Provide intervention and extension based on the results of the end-of-unit assessment while the next unit of study is initiated.	☐ "What knowledge, skills, and dispositions should every student acquire as a result of this unit, this course, or this grade level?" ☐ "How will we know when each student has acquired the essential knowledge and skills?" ☐ "How will we respond when some students do not learn?" ☐ "How will we extend the learning for students who are already proficient?"	

DuFour, R., DuFour, R., Eaker, R., Many, T. W., Mattos, M., & Muhammad, A. (2024). *Learning by doing: A handbook for Professional Learning Communities at Work* (4th ed.). Bloomington, IN: Solution Tree Press.

Matching: Teaching-Assessing-Learning Cycle Components Key

Check all that apply.

Component	To Which Question This Component Applies and Why
Determine essential standards and associated learning targets for the upcoming unit of study.	☑ "What knowledge, skills, and dispositions should every student acquire as a result of this unit, this course, or this grade level?" ☐ "How will we know when each student has acquired the essential knowledge and skills?" ☐ "How will we respond when some students do not learn?" ☐ "How will we extend the learning for students who are already proficient?"
Create the end-of-unit assessment based on what has been determined to be essential.	☐ "What knowledge, skills, and dispositions should every student acquire as a result of this unit, this course, or this grade level?" ☑ "How will we know when each student has acquired the essential knowledge and skills?" ☐ "How will we respond when some students do not learn?" ☐ "How will we extend the learning for students who are already proficient?"
Plan interim assessments that will be used to check on learning within the unit.	☐ "What knowledge, skills, and dispositions should every student acquire as a result of this unit, this course, or this grade level?" ☑ "How will we know when each student has acquired the essential knowledge and skills?" ☐ "How will we respond when some students do not learn?" ☐ "How will we extend the learning for students who are already proficient?"
Deliver and analyze interim assessments.	☐ "What knowledge, skills, and dispositions should every student acquire as a result of this unit, this course, or this grade level?" ☑ "How will we know when each student has acquired the essential knowledge and skills?" ☐ "How will we respond when some students do not learn?" ☐ "How will we extend the learning for students who are already proficient?"

Provide intervention and extension based on the results of interim assessments.	☐	"What knowledge, skills, and dispositions should every student acquire as a result of this unit, this course, or this grade level?"
	☐	"How will we know when each student has acquired the essential knowledge and skills?"
	☑	"How will we respond when some students do not learn?"
	☑	"How will we extend the learning for students who are already proficient?"
Deliver and analyze the end-of-unit assessment.	☐	"What knowledge, skills, and dispositions should every student acquire as a result of this unit, this course, or this grade level?"
	☑	"How will we know when each student has acquired the essential knowledge and skills?"
	☐	"How will we respond when some students do not learn?"
	☐	"How will we extend the learning for students who are already proficient?"
Provide intervention and extension based on the results of the end-of-unit assessment while the next unit of study is initiated.	☐	"What knowledge, skills, and dispositions should every student acquire as a result of this unit, this course, or this grade level?"
	☐	"How will we know when each student has acquired the essential knowledge and skills?"
	☑	"How will we respond when some students do not learn?"
	☑	"How will we extend the learning for students who are already proficient?"

DuFour, R., DuFour, R., Eaker, R., Many, T. W., Mattos, M., & Muhammad, A. (2024). Learning by doing: A handbook for Professional Learning Communities at Work (4th ed.). Bloomington, IN: Solution Tree Press.

Doing the Work: Planning a Teaching-Assessing-Learning Cycle

Component	Processing Questions and Notes
Determine essential standards and associated learning targets for the upcoming unit of study.	For an upcoming unit of study, what are the key standards and learning targets?
Create the end-of-unit assessment based on what has been determined to be essential.	What will be used for the end-of-unit assessment? When will this be delivered?
Plan interim assessments that will be used to check on learning within the unit.	What targets should be checked on before the end of the unit? How and when will those be assessed?
Deliver and analyze interim assessments.	When will interim assessments be analyzed? How will the assessments be able to tell us who is and who is not on track to meet proficiency?

Provide intervention and extension based on the results of interim assessments.	Based on what is being assessed on interim assessments, can we predict some interventions and extensions that may be necessary?
Deliver and analyze the end-of-unit assessment.	When will the assessment be analyzed? How will the assessment be able to tell us who is and who is not on track to meet proficiency?
Provide intervention and extension based on the results of the end-of-unit assessment while the next unit of study is initiated.	Based on what is being assessed in the end-of-unit assessment, can we predict some interventions and extensions that may be necessary?

Doing the Work: Planning a Teaching-Assessing-Learning Cycle Key

Component	Processing Questions and Notes
Determine essential standards and associated learning targets for the upcoming unit of study.	For an upcoming unit of study, what are the key standards and learning targets? Students will be able to do three things: (1) state a claim, (2) provide three pieces of evidence from the text defending the claim, and (3) do so in a coherent paragraph.
Create the end-of-unit assessment based on what has been determined to be essential.	What will be used for the end-of-unit assessment? When will this be delivered? Students will individually produce a written paragraph stating a claim and providing three pieces of evidence. To do this, students will be provided a two-page article on the pros and cons of mandating a maximum forty-hour work week. Students will be provided the article and task in the writing block on X date.
Plan interim assessments that will be used to check on learning within the unit.	What targets should be checked on before the end of the unit? How and when will those be assessed? During week one of the unit, we will ask students to independently state a claim based on the article we are studying that week. During week two of the unit, we will provide students with a claim for an article and ask them to provide three pieces of evidence from the text to defend the claim. During week three of the unit, we will ask students to organize a provided claim and evidence into a coherent paragraph.
Deliver and analyze interim assessments.	When will interim assessments be analyzed? How will the assessments be able to tell us who is and who is not on track to meet proficiency? These will occur each Wednesday, allowing us to review results at our weekly meeting and plan instruction accordingly. We will use a can do/can't do checklist for each assessment.

Provide intervention and extension based on the results of interim assessments.	Based on what is being assessed on interim assessments, can we predict some interventions and extensions that may be necessary?
	These are only assessing one target at a time so we can easily group students by need on that specific skill.
Deliver and analyze the end-of-unit assessment.	When will the assessment be analyzed? How will the assessment be able to tell us who is and who is not on track to meet proficiency?
	We will deliver this assessment on the last Wednesday of the unit so we can analyze data at our weekly team meeting. This assessment will use the same can do/can't do checklist as the interim assessments.
Provide intervention and extension based on the results of the end-of-unit assessment while the next unit of study is initiated.	Based on what is being assessed in the end-of-unit assessment, can we predict some interventions and extensions that may be necessary?
	We will need to develop intervention groups for stating claims, citing evidence, and constructing paragraphs. We may also need to consider developing intervention groups for how to read a text in order to establish a claim and evidence.

Epilogue

We are all unified by our desire to help students thrive. In that spirit, I want to give you my full and heartfelt best wishes for your journey. It is my goal that this resource provides you with some of the tools to support your work in pursuing excellence. I want to leave you with three simple yet foundational concepts.

1. **Every student matters:** Every student who walks through the school doors matters and deserves excellence.

2. **Adults have impact:** We must know that adults make a difference in the lives of the students we serve each and every day.

3. **Research-based actions accelerate learning:** A plethora of relevant research and experience demonstrate what leads to high levels of learning for every student.

We must take these actions, which is where the PLC at Work process was born. If we do not, we are not serving students to the best of our ability.

This may feel heavy, but the PLC at Work process embodies the necessary actions. Don't hold back. Keep your foot on the gas. Get it done. Students are too important not to.

References and Resources

Ainsworth, L. (2015). *Priority standards: The power of focus.* Accessed at www.edweek.org/education/opinion-priority-standards-the-power-of-focus/2015/02 on May 8, 2024.

Akiba, M., & Liang, G. (2016). Effects of teacher professional learning activities on student achievement growth. *Journal of Educational Research, 109*(1), 99–110.

Anderson, S. G., & Olivier, D. F. (2022). A quantitative study of schools as learning organizations: An examination of professional learning communities, teacher self-efficacy, and collective efficacy. *Research Issues in Contemporary Education, 7*(1), 26–51.

Bailey, K., & Jakicic, C. (2012). *Common formative assessment: A toolkit for Professional Learning Communities at Work.* Bloomington, IN: Solution Tree Press.

Bailey, K., & Jakicic, C. (2019). *Make it happen: Coaching with the four critical questions of PLCs at Work.* Bloomington, IN: Solution Tree Press.

Bailey, K., & Jakicic, C. (2023). *Common formative assessment: A toolkit for Professional Learning Communities at Work* (2nd ed.). Bloomington, IN: Solution Tree Press.

Bayewitz, M. D., Cunningham, S. A., Ianora, J. A., Jones, B., Nielsen, M., Remmert, W., et al. (2020). *Help your team: Overcoming common collaborative challenges in a PLC at Work.* Bloomington, IN: Solution Tree Press.

Buffum, A., Mattos, M., & Malone, J. (2018). *Taking action: A handbook for RTI at Work.* Bloomington, IN: Solution Tree Press.

Buffum, A., Mattos, M., & Weber, C. (2012). *Simplifying response to intervention: Four essential guiding principles.* Bloomington, IN: Solution Tree Press.

Conzemius, A. E., & O'Neill, J. (2014). *The handbook for SMART school teams: Revitalizing best practices for collaboration* (2nd ed.). Bloomington, IN: Solution Tree Press.

Cooper, D. (2022). *Rebooting assessment: A practical guide for balancing conversations, performances, and products.* Bloomington, IN: Solution Tree Press.

Depka, E. (2019). *Letting data lead: How to design, analyze, and respond to classroom assessment.* Bloomington, IN: Solution Tree Press.

Dimich, N. (2024). *Design in five: Essential phases to create engaging assessment practice* (2nd ed.). Bloomington, IN: Solution Tree Press.

Dimich, N., Erkens, C., Miller, J., Schimmer, T., & White, K. (2022). *Concise answers to frequently asked questions about assessment and grading.* Bloomington, IN: Solution Tree Press.

Drucker, P. F. (1954). *The practice of management.* New York: Harper & Row.

DuFour, R., DuFour, R., Eaker, R., Many, T. W., Mattos, M., & Muhammad, A. (2024). *Learning by doing: A handbook for Professional Learning Communities at Work* (4th ed.). Bloomington, IN: Solution Tree Press.

DuFour, R., DuFour, R., Eaker, R., Mattos, M., & Muhammad, A. (2021). *Revisiting PLCs at Work: Proven insights for sustained, substantive school improvement* (2nd ed). Bloomington, IN: Solution Tree Press.

Ferriter, W. M. (2020). *The big book of tools for collaborative teams in a PLC at Work.* Bloomington, IN: Solution Tree Press.

Ferriter, W. M., Mattos, M, & Meyer, R. J. (2025). *The big book of tools for RTI at Work.* Bloomington, IN: Solution Tree Press.

Gardner, S., & Albee, D. (2015, February 1). *Study focuses on strategies for achieving goals, resolutions* [Press release]. Accessed at https://scholar.dominican.edu/cgi/viewcontent.cgi?article=1265&context=news-releases on June 5, 2024.

Grant, L. W., Hindman, J., & Stronge, J. (2010). *Planning, instruction, and assessment: Effective teaching practices.* New York: Routledge.

Hall, B. (2022). *Powerful guiding coalitions: How to build and sustain the leadership team in your PLC at Work.* Bloomington, IN: Solution Tree Press.

Hannigan, J., Hannigan, J. D., Mattos, M., & Buffum, A. (2021). *Behavior solutions: Teaching academic and social skills through RTI at Work.* Bloomington, IN: Solution Tree Press.

Harlacher, J. E., Potter, J., & Collins, A. (2024). *Untangling data-based decision making: A problem-solving model to enhance MTSS.* Bloomington, IN: Solution Tree Press.

Hattie, J. (2023). *Visible learning: The sequel 2023—A synthesis of over 2,100 meta-analyses relating to achievement.* New York: Routledge.

Heacox, D. (2002). *Differentiating instruction in the regular classroom: How to reach and teach all learners, grades 3–12.* Minneapolis, MN: Free Spirit.

Hillman, G., & Stalets, M. (2019). *Coaching your classroom: How to deliver actionable feedback to students.* Bloomington, IN: Solution Tree Press.

Höchli, B., Brügger, A., & Messner, C. (2018). How focusing on superordinate goals motivates broad, long-term goal pursuit: A theoretical perspective. *Frontiers in Psychology, 9,* 1879.

Hord, S. (2015). What is an authentic professional learning community? *Journal of Staff Development, 36*(3), 38–39.

Hord, S. M. (1997). *Professional learning communities: Communities of continuous inquiry and improvement.* Accessed at https://sedl.org/pubs/change34/plc-cha34.pdf on August 20, 2024.

Johansen, M. O., Eliassen, S., & Jeno, L. M. (2023). "Why is this relevant for me?": Increasing content relevance enhances student motivation and vitality. *Frontiers in Psychology, 14,* 1184804.

Kise, J. A. G. (2021). *Doable differentiation: Twelve strategies to meet the needs of all learners.* Bloomington, IN: Solution Tree Press.

Kramer, S. V., Sonju, B., Mattos, M., & Buffum, A. (2020). *Best practices at Tier 2: Supplemental interventions for additional student support, elementary.* Bloomington, IN: Solution Tree Press.

Leane, B., & Yost, J. (2022). *Singletons in a PLC at Work: Navigating on-ramps to meaningful collaboration.* Bloomington, IN: Solution Tree Press.

Marzano, R. J. (2003). *What works in schools: Translating research into action.* Arlington, VA: ASCD.

Mattos, M., Buffum, A., Malone, J., Cruz, L. F., Dimich, N., & Schuhl, S. (2024). *Taking action: A handbook for RTI at Work* (2nd ed.). Bloomington, IN: Solution Tree Press.

Mattos, M., DuFour, R., DuFour, R., Eaker, R., & Many, T. W. (2016). *Concise answers to frequently asked questions about Professional Learning Communities at Work*. Bloomington, IN: Solution Tree Press.

Navo, M., & Williams, A. (2022). *Demystifying MTSS: A school and district framework for meeting students' academic and social-emotional needs*. Bloomington, IN: Solution Tree Press.

Nielsen, M. (2024). *The 15-day challenge: Simplify and energize your PLC at Work process*. Bloomington, IN: Solution Tree Press.

Read On Arizona. (2024). *Case studies: Agua Caliente Elementary and Tanque Verde Elementary*. Accessed at https://readonarizona.org/case-studies/TVUSD on April 1, 2024.

Reeves, D. (2020). *Achieving equity and excellence: Immediate results from the lessons of high-poverty, high-success schools*. Bloomington, IN: Solution Tree Press.

Reibel, A. R., Gobble, T., Onuscheck, M., & Twadell, E. (2024). *Beyond PLC lite: Evidence-based teaching and learning in a Professional Learning Community at Work*. Bloomington, IN: Solution Tree Press.

Roberts, M. (2019). *Enriching the learning: Meaningful extensions for proficient students in a PLC at Work*. Bloomington, IN: Solution Tree Press.

Rogers, P., Smith, W. R., Buffum, A., & Mattos, M. (2020). *Best practices at Tier 3: Intensive interventions for remediation, elementary*. Bloomington, IN: Solution Tree Press.

Rogers, P., Smith, W. R., Buffum, A., & Mattos, M. (2020). *Best practices at Tier 3: Intensive interventions for remediation, secondary*. Bloomington, IN: Solution Tree Press.

Satterstrom, P., Kerrissey, M. J., & DiBenigno, J. (2022). *How the best teams keep good ideas alive*. Accessed at https://hbr.org/2022/05/how-the-best-teams-keep-good-ideas-alive on July 16, 2024.

Simms, J. A. (2024). *The Marzano synthesis: A collected guide to what works in K–12 education*. Bloomington, IN: Marzano Resources.

Sloper, C., & Grift, G. (2021). *Collaborative teams that work: The definitive guide to cycles of learning in a PLC*. Bloomington, IN: Solution Tree Press.

Solution Tree. (2024a). *Evidence of excellence: Minnieville Elementary School*. Accessed at www.solutiontree.com/plc-at-work/evidence-of-excellence/minnieville on April 1, 2024.

Solution Tree. (2024b). *PLC at Work success story: Fern Creek High School*. Accessed at https://cloudfront-s3.solutiontree.com/pdf/EOE/SolutionTree_EOE_Fern_Creek.pdf?_ga=2.250626373.2104238624.1712243703-441923646.1689021104 on April 1, 2024.

Sonju, B., Kramer, S. V., Buffum, A., & Mattos, M. (2019). *Best practices at Tier 2: Supplemental interventions for additional student support, secondary*. Bloomington, IN: Solution Tree Press.

Sonju, B., Powers, M., & Miller, S. (2023). *Simplifying the journey: Six steps to schoolwide collaboration, consistency, and clarity in a PLC at Work*. Bloomington, IN: Solution Tree Press.

Spiller, J., & Power, K. (2019). *Leading with intention: Eight areas for reflection and planning in your PLC at Work*. Bloomington, IN: Solution Tree Press.

Tomlinson, C. A. (2017). *How to differentiate instruction in academically diverse classrooms* (3rd ed.). Arlington, VA: ASCD.

Urban, H. (2003). *Life's greatest lessons: 20 things that matter* (4th ed.). New York: Simon & Schuster.

Weichel, M., McCann, B., & Williams, T. (2018). *When they already know it: How to extend and personalize student learning in a PLC at Work*. Bloomington, IN: Solution Tree Press.

Wiggins, G., & McTighe, J. (2005). *Understanding by design* (Expanded 2nd ed.). Arlington, VA: ASCD.

Williams, K. (n.d.). *I thought I was the difference* [Video file]. Accessed at https://unfoldthesoul.com on September 25, 2024.

Wormeli, R. (2018). *Fair isn't always equal: Assessing and grading in the differentiated classroom* (2nd ed.). Portland, ME: Stenhouse.

Yeager, D. S., Henderson, M. D., Paunesku, D., Walton, G. M., D'Mello, S., Spitzer, B. J., et al. (2014). Boring but important: A self-transcendent purpose for learning fosters academic self-regulation. *Journal of Personality and Social Psychology, 107*(4), 559–580.

Zwiers, J., & Crawford, M. (2023). *Academic conversations: Classroom talk that fosters critical thinking and content understandings*. London: Routledge.

Index

A

active learning, 136

agendas, 45

assessments.
See also specific types of
   assessing and responsibility, 114
   critical question two and, 79
   data analysis and, 80
   feedback and, 79–89
   loose and tight elements and, 8
   teaching-assessing-learning cycle components, 135.
      See also teaching-assessing-learning cycle

B

backward design, 79

big ideas of a PLC
   about, 6
   critical questions and, 77, 95, 113
   guiding coalitions and, 26
   teams and, 25, 43, 44

C

categorizing: activities to support interventions and extensions, 116, 118.
   See also extensions; interventions

collaboration, 62

collaborative teams.
See also teams
   about, 43
   activities for, 46–49
   considerations for team success, 45–46
   critical questions of a PLC and, 9, 61–62

discussion questions and next steps resources, 46

doing the work: critical considerations of a collaborative team, 47, 49

extensions and, 114

facilitating professional learning, 47

foundational PLC at Work concepts and, 7–8

reproducibles for, 50–59

role of, understanding, 43–46

scenarios: collaborative teams, 47–48

teaching-assessing-learning cycle and, 134

team goals, 44

collective commitments, 7, 8, 26.
See also values

common assessments, 8, 9.
See also assessments

common formative assessments, 134.
See also assessments

connections, developing, 47

critical question four.
See also critical questions of a PLC

   about, 113

   activities for, 116–118

   discussion questions and next steps resources, 116

   facilitating professional learning, 117

   reproducibles for, 119–130

   scenarios: critical question four in a PLC at Work, 116, 117

   understanding critical question four, 113–115

critical question one.
See also critical questions of a PLC

   about, 61

   activities for, 64–67

   discussion questions and next steps resources, 64

   doing the work: critical question one, 65, 67

   facilitating professional learning, 65

   reproducibles for, 68–75

   scenarios: critical question one in a PLC at Work, 65–66

   understanding critical question one, 61–64

critical question three.
See also critical questions of a PLC

   about, 95

   activities for, 98–101

   discussion questions and next steps resources, 98

   facilitating professional learning, 99

   reproducibles for, 102–111

   scenarios: critical question three in a PLC at Work, 99–100

   understanding critical question three, 96–98

critical question two.
See also critical questions of a PLC

   about, 77

   activities for, 80–83

   discussion questions and next steps resources, 80

   facilitating professional learning, 81

   reproducibles for, 84–93

   scenarios: critical question two in a PLC at Work, 80, 81

   thumbs-up or thumbs down: critical question two in a PLC at Work, 80, 81

   understanding critical question two, 77–79

critical questions of a PLC.
See also specific critical questions of a PLC

   about, 8–9

   matching: teaching-assessing-learning cycle components and the four critical questions, 138, 139–140

   schoolwide behavior teams and, 26

   teaching-assessing-learning cycle and, 44–45, 133, 134

   understanding team structures in a PLC at Work, 26

cross-disciplinary teams, 44.
See also teams

D

data

   considerations for team success, 45–46

   data analysis, 79

doing the work: data analysis, 80–81, 82–83

determining actions: planning how to respond, 99, 100–101

differentiation, 114–115.
    See also critical question four

dissonance, 46

doing the work: critical considerations of a collaborative team, 47, 49.
    See also collaborative teams

doing the work: critical question one, 65, 67.
    See also critical question one

doing the work: data analysis, 80–81, 82–83.
    See also data

doing the work: an extension plan, 116–117, 118.
    See also extensions

doing the work: planning a teaching-assessing-learning cycle, 136, 138.
    See also teaching-assessing-learning cycle

doing the work: practicing the four pillars, 10, 12.
    See also pillars of a PLC

doing the work: a reteaching plan, 99, 101.
    See also reteaching

doing the work: writing team roles, 28–29, 30–31.
    See also teams

E

end-of-unit assessments, 78, 134, 135.
    See also assessments

end-of-unit steps, 135.
    See also teaching-assessing-learning cycle

endurance and identifying priority standards, 62

essential standards
    critical question one and, 62–63
    extensions and, 114
    hit or miss: essential standards, 65, 66–67
    teaching-assessing-learning cycle components, 135

extensions
    categorizing: activities to support interventions and extensions, 116, 117–118
    critical question four and, 113
    essential standards and, 114
    teaching-assessing-learning cycle components, 135

F

facilitating professional learning.
    See professional learning

FAST (frequently discussed, ambitious, specific, and transparent) goals, 44.
    See also goals

feedback, 78–79

flexible grouping, 115

formative assessments, 8.
    See also assessments

foundational PLC at Work concepts
    about, 5
    activities for, 10–12
    discussion questions and next steps resources, 9
    facilitating professional learning, 10
    reproducibles for, 13–23
    understanding the foundational concepts, 5–9

four critical questions.
    See critical questions of a PLC

four pillars.
    See pillars of a PLC

G

goals.
    See also learning goals
    critical question two and, 78
    pillars of a PLC, 7
    professional learning and, 10
    SMART goals, 27, 44
    team goals, 44

guaranteed and viable curriculum, 8, 62

guiding coalitions, 26.
    See also teams

H

hit or miss: essential standards, 65, 66–67.
    See also essential standards

I

interests and differentiation, 115

interventions.
  See also critical question four
    categorizing: activities to support interventions and extensions, 116, 117–118
    site intervention teams, 27, 62
    teaching-assessing-learning cycle components, 135

introduction
    how to use this book, 2–3
    impact of a PLC, 1
    where to start, 3

in-unit steps, 134–135.
  See also teaching-assessing-learning cycle

L

learning goals.
  See also goals
    critical questions of a PLC and, 9, 62, 77, 96
    learning targets and, 63
    teaching-assessing-learning cycle and, 134
    Tier 3, addressing needs in, 98

learning profile and differentiation, 115

learning space, considering, 65

learning stations, 97, 115.
  See also Tier 1, addressing needs in

learning targets
    assessment design and, 78
    critical question one and, 63
    extensions and, 114

leverage and identifying priority standards, 62–63.
  See also essential standards

loose and tight elements, 8

M

matching: responsibilities and teams, 28, 30.
  See also teams

matching: teaching-assessing-learning cycle components and the four critical questions, 136, 137–138.
  See also teaching-assessing-learning cycle

meetings and team success, 45

mission, 6–7.
  See also pillars of a PLC

multi-level learning stations, 115

N

norms, 45

P

pacing guides, 97.
  See also Tier 1, addressing needs in

pillars of a PLC
    about, 6–8
    doing the work: practicing the four pillars, 10, 12
    plus/delta: example the four pillars, 10, 11–12

PLC lite, 6

PLCs at Work
    big ideas of.
      See big ideas of a PLC
    critical questions of.
      See critical questions of a PLC
    foundational concepts of.
      See foundational PLC at Work concepts
    impact of, 1
    loose and tight elements, 8
    pillars of.
      See pillars of a PLC
    research-based actions and, 155
    understanding team structures in a PLC at Work, 25–27

plus/delta: example the four pillars, 10, 11–12

pre-unit steps, 134.
  See also teaching-assessing-learning cycle

professional learning
    active learning and, 136
    connecting to participant roles and school focus, 29
    developing connections, 47

follow-ups to, 99

goals and, 10

learning spaces and, 65

notes, handouts, and slide decks and, 117

processing time and dialogue and, 81

professional learning teams, 7–8, 27. *See also* teams

proficiency, 63

progression ladders, 63

R

ranking: effective teams, 47, 48–49. *See also* collaborative teams; teams

readiness and differentiation, 115

readiness and identifying priority standards, 63

reproducibles for

    analyzing the current reality: collaborative teams, 51

    analyzing the current reality: critical question four, 120

    analyzing the current reality: critical question one, 69

    analyzing the current reality: critical question three, 103

    analyzing the current reality: critical question two, 85

    analyzing the current reality: foundational PLC at Work concepts, 14

    analyzing the current reality: teaching-assessing-learning cycle, 140–141

    analyzing the current reality: teams, 33

    categorizing: activities to support interventions and extensions, 125–126, 127–128

    doing the work: critical considerations of a collaborative team, 58, 59

    doing the work: critical question one, 75

    doing the work: data analysis, 92–93

    doing the work: planning a teaching-assessing-learning cycle, 150–151, 152–153

    doing the work: practicing the four pillars, 23

    doing the work: a reteaching plan, 110, 112, 129–130

    doing the work: writing team roles, 39, 40

    hit or miss: essential standards, 74

    matching: responsibilities and teams, 28, 30

    matching: teaching-assessing-learning cycle components, 146–147, 148–149

    planning how to respond, 108, 109

    plus/delta: the four pillars, 19–20, 21–22

    ranking: effective teams, 56, 57

    scenarios: collaborative teams, 52–53, 54–55

    scenarios: concepts in a PLC at Work key, 17–18

    scenarios: critical question four in a PLC at Work, 121–122, 123–124

    scenarios: critical question one in a PLC at Work, 70–71, 72–73

    scenarios: critical question three in a PLC at Work, 104–105, 106–107

    scenarios: critical question two in a PLC at Work, 86–87, 88–90

    scenarios: foundational PLC at Work concepts, 15–16

    scenarios: teaching-assessing-learning cycle in a PLC at Work, 142–143, 144–145

    scenarios: teams, 33–34, 34–37

    thumbs-up or thumbs down: critical question two in a PLC at Work, 90, 91

    topic processing: collaborative teams, 50

    topic processing: critical question four, 119

    topic processing: critical question one, 68

    topic processing: critical question three, 102

    topic processing: critical question two, 84

    topic processing: foundational PLC at Work concepts, 13

    topic processing: teaching-assessing-learning cycle, 139

    topic processing: teams, 32

response to intervention (RTI), 95, 96. *See also* interventions

reteaching
- doing the work: an extension plan, 116–117, 118
- doing the work: a reteaching plan, 99, 101
- Tier 1, addressing needs in, 97

S

scenarios: collaborative teams, 47–48.
See also collaborative teams

scenarios: critical question four in a PLC at Work, 116, 117.
See also critical question four

scenarios: critical question one in a PLC at Work, 65–66.
See also critical question one

scenarios: critical question three in a PLC at Work, 99–100.
See also critical question three

scenarios: critical question two in a PLC at Work, 80, 81.
See also critical question two

scenarios: foundational PLC at Work concepts, 10–11.
See also foundational PLC at Work concepts

scenarios: teaching-assessing-learning cycle in a PLC at Work, 136, 137.
See also teaching-assessing-learning cycle

scenarios: teams, 28, 29.
See also teams

schoolwide behavior teams, 26–27, 62.
See also teams

scope and sequence, 63–64

singletons, 8

site intervention teams, 27, 62.
See also interventions; teams

SMART (specific, measurable, achievable, realistic, and time bound) goals, 27, 44.
See also goals

standards, 62–63.
See also essential standards

T

teacher collaborative teams, 27.
See also collaborative teams; teams

teaching-assessing-learning cycle
- about, 133
- activities for, 136–138
- critical questions of a PLC and, 44–45
- discussion questions and next steps resources, 136
- doing the work: planning a teaching-assessing-learning cycle, 136, 138
- facilitating professional learning, 136
- knowing the teaching-assessing-learning cycle, 134–135
- matching: teaching-assessing-learning cycle components and the four critical questions, 136, 137–138
- reproducibles for, 139–153
- scenarios: teaching-assessing-learning cycle in a PLC at Work, 136, 137

teams.
See also collaborative teams
- about, 25
- activities for, 28–31
- considerations for team success, 45–46
- discussion questions and next steps resources, 28
- doing the work: writing team roles, 28–29, 30–31
- facilitating professional learning, 29
- guiding coalitions, 26
- matching: responsibilities and teams, 28, 30
- ranking: effective teams, 47, 48–49
- reproducibles for, 32–41
- scenarios: teams, 28, 29
- schoolwide behavior teams, 26–27
- site intervention teams, 27
- teacher collaborative teams, 27
- teaching-assessing-learning cycle and, 133
- team goals, 46
- understanding team structures in a PLC at Work, 25–27

three big ideas.
See big ideas of a PLC

thumbs-up or thumbs down: critical question two in a PLC at Work, 80, 82.
See also critical question two

Tier 1, addressing needs in, 97.
See also critical question three

Tier 2, addressing needs in, 97–98.
See also critical question three

Tier 3, addressing needs in, 98.
See also critical question three

tiered assignments, 115

U

Urban, H., 46

V

values, 6, 7

vertical teams, 44.
See also teams

vision, 6, 7

The Big Book of Tools for RTI at Work™
William M. Ferriter, Mike Mattos, and Rob J. Meyer

Whether you're in collaborative teams identifying grade-level standards, school leadership teams assessing Tier 2 interventions, or intervention teams helping at-risk students, this book offers educators the targeted tools necessary to create a highly effective multitiered system of supports (MTSS) that can ensure high levels of learning for every student.
BKG132

Taking Action, Second Edition
Mike Mattos, Austin Buffum, Janet Malone, Luis F. Cruz, Nicole Dimich, and Sarah Schuhl

The second edition of the bestseller *Taking Action* offers a step-by-step guide that defines—tier by tier—the essential actions of the guiding coalition, teacher teams, and intervention team. Educators will delve deeper into how to leverage the PLC at Work® process to create a highly effective multitiered system of supports.
BKG136

Behavior Solutions
John Hannigan, Jessica Djabrayan Hannigan, Mike Mattos, and Austin Buffum

Take strategic action to close the systemic behavior gap with the support of *Behavior Solutions*. Foster social-emotional learning (SEL) by utilizing the PLC at Work® and RTI at Work™ processes to boost student metacognition and create an action plan for meeting their psychological needs.
BKF891

Make It Happen
Kim Bailey and Chris Jakicic

Discover powerful instructional coaching tools, strategies, and processes aligned to the four critical questions of Professional Learning Communities at Work®. Ensure all collaborative teams in your PLC school are engaged in the right work to support student learning.
BKF840

Beyond PLC Lite
Anthony R. Reibel, Troy Gobble, Mark Onuscheck, and Eric Twadell

Designed for teachers and leaders who want to disrupt the status quo, bust out of PLC Lite, and persistently pursue a culture of continuous improvement, this book carries it all. It emphasizes creating a student-centered approach to teaching and learning in a PLC that prioritizes student agency and efficacy.
BKF913

Solution Tree | Press
a division of Solution Tree

Visit SolutionTree.com or call 800.733.6786 to order.

Tremendous, tremendous, tremendous!

The speaker made me do some very deep internal reflection about the **PLC process** and the personal responsibility I have in making the school improvement process work **for ALL kids.**

—Marc Rodriguez, teacher effectiveness coach, Denver Public Schools, Colorado

PD Services

Our experts draw from decades of research and their own experiences to bring you practical strategies for building and sustaining a high-performing PLC. You can choose from a range of customizable services, from a one-day overview to a multiyear process.

Book your PLC PD today!
888.763.9045

Solution Tree